DROPSHIPPING

Beginners' Guide to Starting and Making Money

Online in the E-Commerce Industry

(2022 Crash Course For beginners)

Table of Contents

INTRODUCTION

Making genuine money online has never been easier, especially with Shopify drop shipping. Once you have the money to build up a website, name, and host it, purchase in and store huge quantities of products, and deal with the hassle of filling and shipping orders. Drop shipping takes care of everything by removing the hassle and hard work from your hands and depositing the funds into your account overnight.

Drop shipping is a profitable business concept that allows you to buy items from a distributor, wholesaler, or other manufacturer and ship them straight to your customers. This allows you to speed up the process and immediately deliver the items to your customer from the supplier's warehouse rather than selling them to your customer and delivering them from your customer's warehouse.

In a nutshell, drop shipping allows you to act as a "middleman," selling to the general public without holding any inventory. The risks are substantially reduced; all you have to do is discover suppliers, market the items, and submit orders to the providers. They provide you with the difference between the cost of your items and the amount you sell them for, allowing you to effortlessly generate money with little risk and work.

Drop shipping is not a new money-making concept; it has been used in some form or another since long before the internet was invented. The Internet only enables, accelerates, and expands the market for more individuals to purchase and trade goods and money.

You've arrived at the correct site if you want to learn everything there is to know about drop shipping Shopify model 2021 and how to make money rapidly this year. I hope you appreciate this book and that it is useful to you. I want to see you on the winning side of life.

CHAPTER ONE

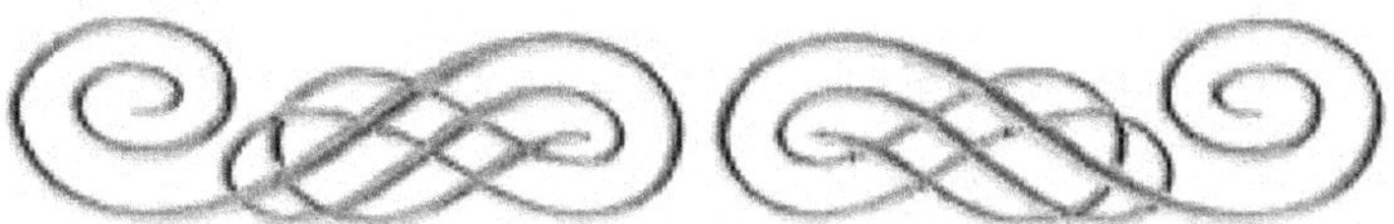

WHAT IS DROPSHIPPING

rop shipping is a retail fulfilment method in which a shop does not have the things it offers in stock. Rather, when a shop sells a product using the drop-shipping model, it purchases the item from a third party and has it sent directly to the customer. As a result, the dealer does not have to deal with the items in person. The most striking similarity between drop shipping and the traditional retail model is that the selling merchant does not stock or hold stock. Rather, the seller purchases goods from a third party, often a manufacturer or wholesaler, to satisfy orders as they come in.

HOW DOES SHOPIFY'S DROP SHIPPING WORK?

Two of the most well-known methods for drop shipping on Shopify are to use a supplier information catalogue to find a supplier in North America or anyplace else on the earth, or to use a Shopify app to link you and your business to a large number of suppliers. Why is Shopify such an excellent platform for drop shipping?
To be quite honest, I feel that Shopify is the greatest option for you - a wonderful success with shipping down. Because I'm not one of those gurus who will shake his thoughts without asking them, I'll show you why Shopify is fantastic this way. So, what makes Shopify a good shipping platform? To begin with, it allows you to have a full conventional plug-and-play business without having to master any programming or design abilities.

You may be a complete newcomer, like myself, and yet make a lot of money. You must create your store, add the best-selling items from the Aliexpress marketplace, add great photographs, and establish your pricing before you can start selling like a pro. Best of all, you will receive a free 14-day trial. As a result, you won't have to worry about making large upfront payments or investing a large sum of money. Once you've decided on a niche and the products you'll offer, you'll start developing your store. Simply enter your email address and click the "Start" button, after which you must enter your password and the name of the business. The name of the business will now appear at the top of your web browser. Nonetheless, I strongly advise you to obtain your domain name to make your website appear more professional, and I teach you how to do so along with my shop link with your store name. When it comes to your storage name, it should be sensible and obvious; it should relate to your specialty and brand, so don't just call it a random name or business name; instead, give it a name related to your brand or specialization. Then you can set up your business, wait a few minutes, and everything will be installed automatically for you. And, with the sweep of a magic wand, your shop is full!

OBERLO

I have something I need to talk to you about before we send the hammer packing. It's known as the Shopify Oberlo app. Oberlo is a fantastic tool that allows you to import a big number of aliexpress.com items directly into your business with only a few clicks. It imports everything, including photographs and information, and links the product to the AliExpress marketplace, allowing you to buy the goods from AliExpress in a few clicks when someone orders the product from your website. As a wise reader, I'm sure you're thinking that if Oberlo can accomplish all of this, it's possible that some genius built and other programmers that can just cool down your entire Amazon / Shopify experience. Who wouldn't want to sit back and relax when automated equipment is functioning smoothly? What I'm about to do to you isn't science fiction; several applications may make your job less stressful while also providing you with constant income. Here are a few examples:

CHECKOUT IMPROVEMENT: This software, as the name suggests, specializes in increasing things... The primary function is to increase social media conversions. It will empower you to seize the delicious chances that social media offers. It also gives your consumers great discounts for sharing on Facebook or Twitter, such as 20% off. It's fantastic and simple to use.

CONVERSION: You can simply discover it on the App Store Shopify. And this software is a marketing tool in general, allowing you to send follow-ups, animated emails, newsletters, and receipts. Typically, I use this application to generate Shopify receipts. This tool is quite useful, and I strongly advise you to use it to increase your sales. I provide a comprehensive course titled... And it is, indeed, AMAZING.

PRODUCT UPSELL: Do you wish to play Santa Claus and enjoy the holiday season to gain more consumers and profits? Then this software is ideal for you! During unique holidays, you might provide tailored discounts to your clients.

PERSONALIZATION: This software incorporates relevant retail information and increases your sales. It simply allows you to bring your flair to your store. It's a very cool programmer that enables numerous tweaks that would not otherwise be available.

Product Evaluations: Do you know what they prefer to hear about other individuals who bought the same goods before they buy them? It is no longer a secret that customer evaluations may help or hurt a company's reputation. It essentially allows you to add ratings and reviews to your product page so that the specifics of your customer reviews do not seem empty when you first launch. I'll walk you through my setting and demonstrate how to use these items most efficiently.

THE BENEFITS OF DROP SHIPPING

Drop shipping is a fantastic business strategy for budding business visionaries to start with because it is readily available. Drop shipping allows you to quickly test varied business ideas with little downsides, allowing you to become acquainted with learning more about how to identify and sell high-demand items. Here are a few of the reasons why drop shipping is such a popular business concept.

1. There is a lower requirement for capital.

The most obvious advantage of drop shipping is that it allows you to create an online business store without having to invest thousands of dollars in stock upfront. Traditionally, merchants have had to tie up large sums of cash to acquire merchandise. You don't need to buy any items using the drop shipping model until you've already done the sale and been paid by your client. It is feasible to start sourcing items and delivering a profitable drop shipping business with absolutely no money and no large upfront stock commitments. Furthermore, because you are not committed to selling through any stock purchased upfront, as in a typical retail firm, there is less risk involved with starting a drop shipping store.

2. To begin, keep it simple.

When you don't have to manage real things, running an e-commerce firm becomes a lot easier. With drop shipping, you don't have to worry about:
- Managing or funding a distribution facility
- Your requests will be packed and sent.
- Inventory is being monitored for bookkeeping purposes.
- Returns and incoming shipments are processed.
- Constantly requesting items and monitoring stock levels

3. Low operating expenses

Your overhead expenses are very cheap because you don't need to handle stock acquisition or deal with a distribution center. Indeed, many effective drop shipping companies are managed as locally established enterprises, requiring little more than a workstation and a few recurring fees to function. These costs will most likely rise as you grow, but they will still be affordable in comparison to typical physical firms.4. Adaptable work location

A drop shipping business may be conducted from almost any location that has an internet connection. You can run and manage your business for as long as you can properly communicate with suppliers and clients.

5. A diverse product line to market

You can provide a selection of trending products to your potential consumers because you don't have to pre-purchase the items you sell. If your suppliers have anything in stock, you may make it accessible for purchase on your online store at no extra cost.

6. Easier to test

Drop shipping is a beneficial fulfilment approach for both opening a new store and for business owners looking to test the appetite of customers for more items, such as accessories or whole new product offerings. The main benefit of drop shipping is, once again, the ability to list and perhaps offer items before focusing on acquiring a large amount of stock.

7. Easier to scale

If you have a typical retail business and receive multiple times the number of inquiries, you will need to accomplish more than three times the quantity of work.

By employing drop shipping providers, the majority of the effort to handle more requests will be borne by the suppliers, allowing you to expand with less development anguish and slower labor. Sales expansion will always need more labor, particularly with client help, but firms that employ drop shipping scale exceptionally well when compared to standard e-commerce business operations.

Drop shipping's disadvantages

All of the benefits we mentioned before make drop shipping an appealing option for anybody starting an online company or looking to expand their present product offers. In any case, drop shipping, like other techniques, has its downsides. As a rule, accommodation and adaptation have major drawbacks. Here are a few flaws to think about.

1. Low profit margins

Low margins are the most difficult aspect of working in a highly competitive vertical drop shipping business. Because it is so simple to start, and the overhead expenditures are so little, many rivals open up shop and offer items at rock-bottom prices in order to create cash. They may work on minuscule margins since they have invested so little in starting the firm.

Typically, these merchants will have low-quality websites and poor (if any) customer service, which you may exploit to differentiate your firm. However, this will not stop clients from comparing their prices to yours. This growth in a very competitive market will quickly reduce possible total profits in a specialty. Fortunately, you can mitigate this problem significantly by selecting a niche/vertical that is suitable for drop shipping. In the next chapters, we'll go over how to do just that.

2. Stock market fluctuations

When you carry all of your own items, it's often simple to keep track of what's in and out of stock. In any event, when you're sourcing from many stockrooms that are also fulfilling demands for other suppliers, stock might fluctuate on a regular basis. Fortunately, there are currently a plethora of programmers that allow you to coordinate with suppliers. Drop shippers should be able to "go along" requests to suppliers with a click or two, and they should be able to see how much stock the supplier has at all times. Some e-commerce sites also allow merchants to take automated actions when a supplier's supply reaches zero. For example, if a product is no longer available, you may instantly unpublished it or keep it disseminated while setting the quantity to zero.

3. Shipping complication

If you deal with a variety of suppliers, as most drop shippers do, the items on your online shop will be obtained from a variety of drop shippers. This raises your shipping prices. Assume a client sends a request for three items, all of which are only available from independent vendors. You'll incur three different shipping expenses for sending everything to the customer, but it's probably not a good idea to pass this cost on to the client. Furthermore, even when it makes logical to include these costs, computerizing these computations might be difficult.

4. Mistakes by suppliers

Have you ever been accused of anything that wasn't your fault, yet you still needed to accept responsibility for the blunder? Indeed, even the greatest drop shipping providers make mistakes while fulfilling orders—errors for which you must accept responsibility and apologies.

Furthermore, mediocre and low-quality suppliers may bring constant disappointment due to missing items, mishandled shipping, and low-quality printing, which can affect your company's reputation.

5. Limited branding and personalization

Drop shipping, unlike custom produced items or print on demand, does not allow you a lot of control over the product itself. The supplier, for the most part, brands and packages the product that is outsourced. A few suppliers can accommodate your company's product revisions; nonetheless, the supplier has the greatest power over the product itself. Any advancements or improvements to the product itself normally necessitate a basic request quantity in order to be appropriate and moderate for the maker.

FREQUENTLY ASKED QUESTIONS ABOUT DROP SHIPPING

Throughout the rest of this book, we'll go over all of the necessary steps to start a profitable drop shipping business. Before we go any further, it's important to answer a handful of common questions we hear regarding drop shipping and how it works, especially in 2021.

How much money do I need to start my drop shipping business?

Despite the fact that it is difficult to predict the exact costs for every particular business, there are a few things that every drop shipping business owner should spend money on to get started. Here's a quick rundown of the major costs.

A web-based shop

To create and host an online business, you'll need to select a social networking platform, an e-commerce platform, or a web designer. We strongly advise you to open a Shopify store. You'll be able to connect with ecommerce sites to conveniently source items, and you'll receive access to a variety of subjects and free branding materials to help you get your business up and running quickly. It's tough to establish confidence with clients if you don't have your own domain name. While there are several top-level domains available (for example, example. Shop, example.co), we recommend looking for a business name. Despite the fact that drop shipping allows you to have a minor involvement in dealing with your general product index, you should set aside money, as well as a little time, to test the items you plan to offer. If you don't, you risk posting a product with an overwhelming number of flaws or faults, which will result in disgruntled customers and a lot of time spent processing returns and reimbursements. Some may even post a negative review, which may harm your "company credibility" in the eyes of other clients.

How do drop shippers make money?

Drop shipping companies act as product curators, selecting the best mix of items to promote to customers. Remember that promoting/marketing is an investment you make in both time and money to assist potential customers in discovering, evaluating, and purchasing the right product. You'll also need to factor in the cost of providing customer service if there's a product or shipment issue. Last but not least, the first price at which your provider offers the goods. This is why suppliers feel at ease with having drop shippers market their items for them— drop shipping retailers generate more sales that the supplier would have passed up in any event. To earn a profit with your drop shipping business, figure out how much it costs you to "procure" a customer and then price your items accordingly.

Is drop shipping a legitimate industry?

Drop shipping is primarily a fulfilment mechanism that is used by many global businesses and is completely legal. As with any business, meeting client needs and developing a brand that resonates with the right audience is still critical to long range success. This question is frequently asked because to a misunderstanding of how drop shipping works. Most retail establishments do not sell things that they manufacture. Drop shipping takes this curated method and turns it into a customer satisfaction model suitable for an internet business. There are, clearly, more important things you must do in order to keep your business lawful.

Consult a legal counsel who specializes in these concerns to ensure you're conducting business legally inside your jurisdiction.

Is drop shipping worth it, despite all of its difficulties in 2021?

As previously said, drop shipping is not an easy, stress-free technique to develop a successful online business — hard work is always required to start a business. The approach has several clear advantages, but it also has a number of inherent flaws that must be addressed. In order to be successful in your drop shipping business in 2021, we'll look at these problems and how to effectively solve them. Fortunately, with some careful thinking and preparation, the majority of these barriers can be overcome and will not prevent you from developing a healthy, profitable drop shipping business.

CHAPTER TWO

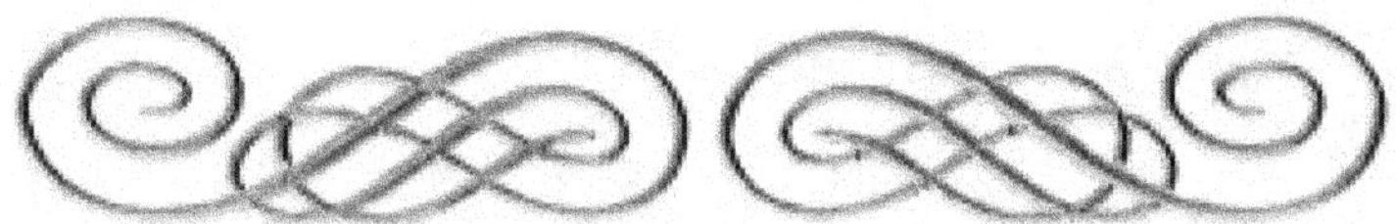

THE SUPPLY CHAIN AND THE FULFILLMENT PROCESS

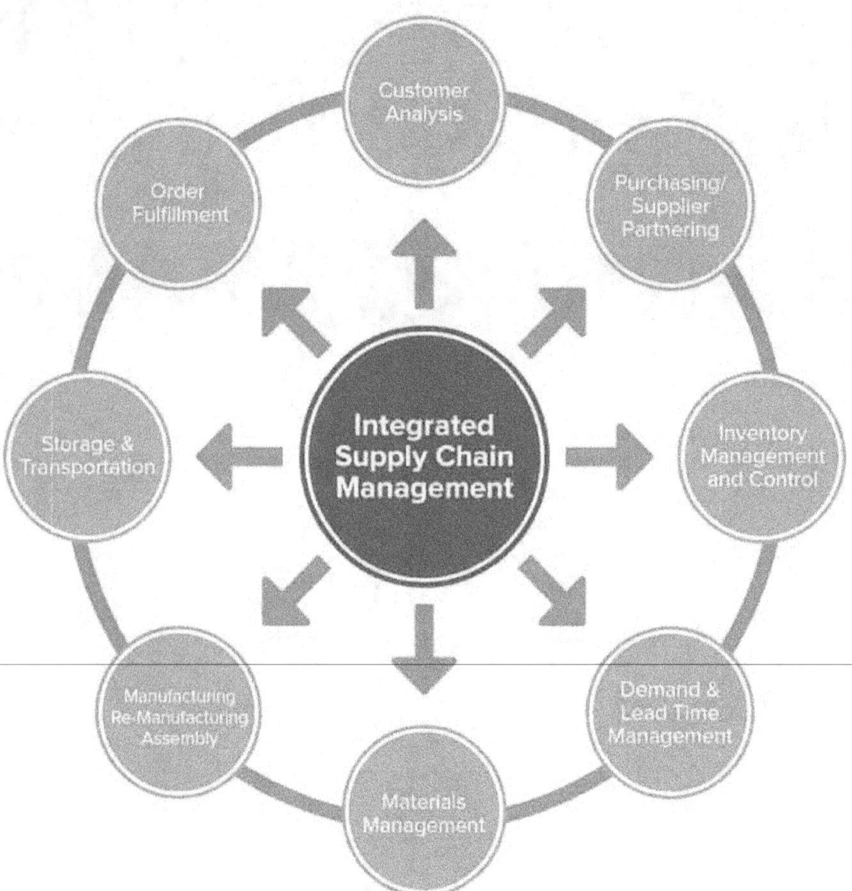

The word "supply chain" refers to the journey of a commodity from conception to manufacturing and, eventually, into the hands of a consumer. When we spoke with hard-core distribution chain gurus, we were told that a company's supply chain extends to manufacturing the materials necessary to make an item (such as oil and rubber). But it's rather intense. We don't need to get that specific for this guide. You must evaluate the three key participants in the drop shipping supply chain: manufacturers, distributors, and retailers.

AND NOW FOR THE FUN PART:

Manufacturers

Manufacturers create the product, and the majority of them do not sell it directly to the market. They also sell in bulk to wholesalers and retailers.

The simplest approach to acquire things for resale is directly from the vendor, but most of them have minimum buying conditions that you must follow. Frequently, you will need to keep the items and then re-ship them when delivering them to customers. Because of these factors, purchasing straight from a wholesaler is frequently more convenient.

Wholesalers

Wholesalers buy in bulk from suppliers, mark them up somewhat, and then sell to public resale distributors. These are often significantly lower than those required by a manufacturer if they have minimum quantities to purchase. Wholesalers typically acquire items from dozens, if not hundreds, of vendors and specialize in a certain sector or niche. Most are strictly wholesalers, selling exclusively to retailers and not directly to the general public.

Retailers

A retailer is somebody who sells things at a discount to the general public directly. You are a retailer if you run a firm that fulfils orders through drop shipping providers.
It is "drop shipping" on your behalf if a manufacturer is prepared to send his items straight to your consumer. Similarly, a retail distributor may offer drop ship, however, the price would be more than that of a wholesaler because it does not buy directly from the vendor.
Just because someone looks to be a "drop shipper" does not imply that you are receiving it at a discounted rate. Simply put, it implies that the corporation is delivering items on your behalf. To receive the greatest costs, you should engage directly with a reputable wholesaler or distributor, which we shall discuss in detail in the following chapter.

HOW DOES DROPSHIPPING WORK?

The Ordering Procedure

Now that you know who the essential participants are, let's take a look at how a drop shipped order is handled. To demonstrate, we will use an order placed with our hypothetical shop, Phone Outlet, an online retailer that specialized in mobile accessories.

Telephone Outlet obtains all of its items from a wholesaler known as wholesale accessories.

Here's an example of how the entire ordering process may look:

STEP 1: The consumer contacts the Phone Outlet and puts an order.

Mr. George requires a cover for his new smartphone and orders one from a Phone Outlet's online site. A few things happen as soon as the order is approved: Phone Outlet and Mr. George both receive an email confirmation (likely identical) of the new order produced by the shop programmer. Mr. George's money is collected during the checkout process and paid immediately into the Phone Outlet bank account.

STEP 2 – Phone Accessory Plug-In Order is placed with Your Supplier. For wholesale accessories, this step is generally as simple as forwarding an email order confirmation to a salesperson. Entire Accessories has a Phone Outlet credit card on file and will charge it for the full purchase amount, including any delivery or handling fees.

Note: While most advanced drop shippers may need automated uploading of XML orders (a standard inventory file format) or the option to manually place orders online, using emails is the most preferred approach to place orders with drop shipping providers since it is straightforward and quick to use.

STEP 3 – Purchase Wholesale Accessories delivering the order if the item is in stock and the wholesaler has paid the Phone Outlet card successfully. The wholesale accessories must pick up the order and deliver it directly to the consumer.
While the cargo is sent from Wholesale Accessories, the Phone Outlet's name and address will show on the return address label, as well as its logo on the invoice and packing slip. Once the shipping has been completed, Wholesale Accessories must inform Phone Outlet with an invoice and a tracking number.

It's worth noting that the turnaround time for drop shipped orders is frequently faster than you'd expect. Most high-quality suppliers can get an order out the door within a few hours, allowing retailers to promote same-day shipping even when employing a drop shipping source.

STEP 4– The shipping client is notified by Phone Outlet.

Phone Outlet must transmit the tracking information to the consumer after receiving the tracking number, most likely using an email system integrated into the online store. The order has been sent, the invoice has been issued, and the client has been notified that the order and delivery procedure is complete. The advantage (or loss) to Phone Outlet is the difference between what is charged to Mr. George and what it paid for, which is Wholesale Accessories.

Drop shippers Are Almost Unnoticed

The drop shipper is completely unseen to the end customer, despite its critical role in the ordering and fulfilment process. Only the Phone Outlet's return address and branding are displayed on the shipment once it has been dispatched. When Mr. George' receives the incorrect merchandise, he calls Phone Outlet, which then works behind the scenes with Wholesale Accessories to have the correct item shipped out. There is no drop shipping wholesaler to the final client. The only obligation is for goods storage and delivery. Everything else-marketing, website development, customer service, and so on is the responsibility of the dealer.

CHAPITRE THREE

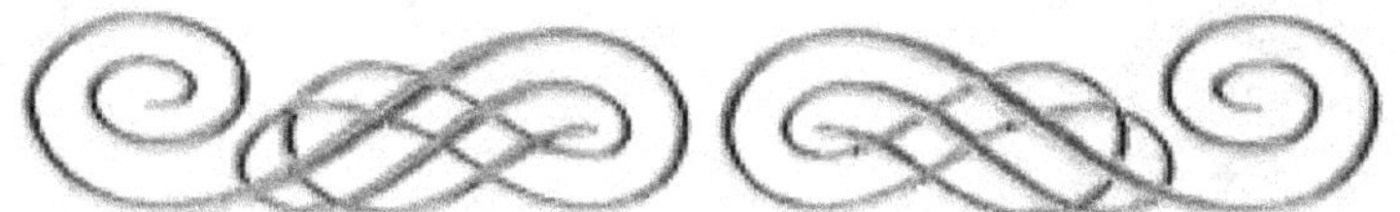

I t may be tough to choose a source for your drop shipping business, but knowing that many providers have been doing it for many years will assist. Some companies control big market sectors, which may be the finest method to start your new firm because the things you sell are already well recognized and respected in the market. You may have to reduce your profit margins or operate in a limited fashion, and you must carefully understand each company's terms and conditions, but each one provides a back door into a rich long-term business. Not every drop shipper is made equal, and you want to be sure that you select the correct source to ensure the success of your business. There are some items that your supplier requires, and others that are less critical but handier.

Some things you want from your supplier are knowledgeable representatives the supplier commits himself to a specific person dedicated to your account, they invest in technologically sophisticated items; how you place your orders; and where they are situated.

There are various methods for locating a reputable drop shipping source. When you get to suppliers, keep in mind that they might be the key to discovering the correct provider, even if they don't meet your demands. Also, ask each provider you approach if they can point you on the correct path for contacting a supplier who is a good fit for your company. Because they work in the industry, they are more willing to assist and provide knowledge. Social networking is another technique to boost your chances of finding a suitable service to deal with. A family member, friend, or acquaintance who works in the business or knows someone who works for the firm might occasionally bind you. Even if it leads to a deadlock, any lead is a good lead. The most often utilized vendors.

Suppliers have a wide range of alternatives to choose from. Given that we want to discover a supplier that is structured, has the resources and is devoted to what they do, you should start with a supplier who has established a brand for itself and the product they sell rather than a supplier and product that are not as well known to the general public.

Here are four of the better alternatives:

SHOPIFY

Shopify is one of the largest online e-commerce platforms, however, it only contains a portion of its platform. Shopify allows you to set up your account and drop shop, as well as generate a solid hosting and domain name, so you can be up and running in less than 30 minutes. You may then select your service providers– Amazon and eBay are two of the most prominent vendors, and you may link with them using Shopify to advertise their items on your website. Shopify provides a one-of-a-kind e-commerce platform as well as a variety of payment choices. It implies you can offer these things to your clients–the more options you have, the more likely you are to attract customers.

Shopify has been in business for a long time and provides a comprehensive package that allows you to establish your business fast and effortlessly. It's simple to get started–just go to your website and select either free or premium hosting–you may upgrade later if you don't want to continue with the free one. You will be given detailed instructions on how to construct and run your website. If it is hosted someplace, you can utilize goods from their platform on your website.

This allows you to collect cash from your clients in a safe manner while still meeting all regulatory standards for data storage and personal data security.

Shopify is one of Amazon's recommended solutions since it is one of the simplest to use and produces excellent results. It may be nearly totally customized for you, allowing you to construct a real one-of-a-kind shop. In brief, Shopify will adapt to your demands so that you do not appear identical to all other online companies. Building on it is a fantastic starting point because the majority of your effort and research has already been done for you. Using Amazon and eBay as drop shippers for your business is a secure idea because they have both already developed their brands and reputations.

PRIVATE LABELLING

When you first start a firm, you may focus on developing well-known and renowned brands, and a private label can help you choose a distributor or supplier. The first stage in starting a business is to manufacture things that are durable and pleasing to the buyer. The second and most important step is to introduce yourself to existing and prospective clients. The more individuals who recognize your brand, the greater your sales will be. You may assist with this by picking manufacturers or suppliers who provide your items under private brands. This works by letting the customer place their purchase with you, which you then transmit to the supplier, who then delivers the product directly to the client. In normal circumstances, the manufacturer's name and address appear on the return, but with the Private Label, it is yours. It guarantees that the consumer is aware that the goods came from you and will contact you if they have any complaints or questions. This allows you to develop your business name, but it is up to you to employ reputable vendors and deliver excellent customer service. Providers are typically delighted to employ private label advertisements since it frees them from having to deal with client complaints.

To summarize, a private label makes sense if you want to get your brand out there and expand your business without relying on Amazon or eBay's success. Finding a firm may take a little longer since it enables time to perform the job yourself and ensure that you deal with the best supplier, but you can frequently make more money by taking responsibility for customer service and being able to negotiate the pricing the provider provides.

Amazon Fulfillment by Amazon Amazon is a household name, and FBA is the solution for anybody who is starting or has already started a business. It allows you to use Amazon's strong reputation as a reference for your business without incurring any costs. Unfortunately, this is not a drop shipping-specific programmer since you must be able to transport actual items to an Amazon Fulfillment Center–when an order is accepted by Amazon, you complete the order using their delivery choices.

Nonetheless, there is no need to pay for warehouse inventory because Amazon will keep it all for you and manage the packaging and shipping for a nominal cost. To summarize, Amazon FBA is not the first choice for a company looking to implement drop shipping. Nonetheless, finding a reliable wholesale dealer that does not sell but gives a fair price on the goods might be a smart choice. If you want to take advantage of these costs without having to invest in warehouse and personnel to ship for you, this is a potential business option. Arbitrage in retail another technique that does not completely fail. Finding things at the correct price for the advantage of reselling is what retail arbitrage is all about. This implies that you will want funds as well as a good carrier to be linked with. This is an excellent approach to saving time and space by utilizing Amazon FBA. The key is to discover the appropriate items at the right price, and you may take advantage of wholesalers. Select the correct goods with care, and don't be afraid to start small.

Drop shipping may work extremely well in conjunction with retail arbitration, and you can make a lot of money. The establishment of a supply network

In the context of a typical firm, the construction and management of a supply chain do not imply drop shipping. Nonetheless, it aids in the expansion of your suppliers and providers. The supplier is in charge of determining pricing, payment conditions, delivery dates, and even the availability of an item. Good ties with your distributor can help you get lower costs, more flexible terms, and more usability. You may strengthen your relationship with your supplier by doing the following: -pay on time to gain confidence and become a trusted client; -set clear and attainable goals when they ask for an estimate of your goods that you want them to deliver in a given time; -be aware that they have other clients and that they do not belong solely to you; -learn what they require from you to expedite their order.

Seek out and collaborate with the proper providers. Before you start looking for the proper suppliers, it's critical to learn how to tell the difference between a legitimate wholesale supplier and a retail business. A reputable wholesaler purchases a supplier's inventory and offers considerably better pricing than a seller. How to Recognize a Scam Drop shipping Wholesaler There may be a variety of bogus wholesalers. Unfortunately, many contemporary wholesalers aren't very adept at marketing and might be difficult to discover. That is, the phone one exposes more results in your searches than the actual ones.

Use the following ways to determine whether a wholesaler is legitimate:

PAYMENTS ARE MADE INDEFINITELY.

A genuine wholesaler will not charge you a monthly fee to buy from them. If a recurrent service or membership charge is requested, the distributor is most likely a swindler. Check to check whether there is a list of vendors. These are directories that provide wholesaler lists that have been verified and categorized by product type or industry. They charge a one-time or monthly fee for information access. If you want true wholesale rates, you must apply for a wholesale account, which requires you to demonstrate that you are running a legitimate business and to wait for approval before making an order. If your "wholesale business" provides wholesale pricing to the general public, they are not genuine; they are high-inflation distributors of products, and lawful bulk charges, such as:

ACCORDING TO THE ORDER

Most legal drop shippers charge a drop shipping fee for every order, which can range from \$2 to \$5 or more. It is determined by the order's size and scale.
Because individual purchases are more expensive to bundle and transport than bulk orders, this is an industry norm.
When looking for suppliers, it is critical to understand how to discern between legal wholesale suppliers and retail establishments that are wholesale providers. A reputable wholesaler purchases directly from the supplier and May frequently offer you even better discounts.

HOW TO RECOGNIZE FALSE DROP SHIPPING WHOLESALERS

Depending on where you go, you're likely to stumble across a slew of "fake" wholesalers. Unfortunately, bogus wholesalers are generally terrible at marketing and have a more difficult time with it. As a result, non-genuine wholesalers, mainly intermediaries, may surface more frequently in your searches, so be cautious. The following strategies can assist you in determining whether a wholesale provider is legitimate:
They need continuing payments–true wholesalers do not charge their clients a monthly fee for the pleasure of doing business and purchasing merchandise. A monthly membership fee or service charge requested by a supplier may not be legal. It is critical to distinguish between manufacturer and seller directories in this context. Supplier directories (which we shall explore shortly) are wholesale supplier directories that are arranged by product type or industry and are checked to verify that genuine suppliers are included. Most directories demand a fee, either one-time or recurring, thus this should not be interpreted as an indication that the directory is unlawful.

They market to the general public–to receive true wholesale pricing, you'll need to apply for a wholesale account, verify you're a legitimate firm and get accepted before you place your first order. Any supermarket merchant that sells items to the general public at "wholesale pricing" is essentially a manufacturer selling overpriced products. However, the following are some legitimate drop shipping expenses that you are likely to encounter:

FEES FOR EACH ORDER

Many drop shippers might charge a per-order drop shipping cost that can range from $2 to $6 or more, depending on the quantity and volume of delivering items. Because each order packing and shipping costs are substantially greater than sending a bulk purchase, this is the industry norm.

MINIMUM ORDER QUANTITY

The majority of wholesalers will offer the minimal quantity–the very lowest amount to purchase when you first shop–for a first-time order. It's all about converting window shoppers into paying consumers. This may be quite profitable for drop shippers–for example, a wholesaler has a minimum purchase of $500 and an average order of around $150. It's pointless to spend $500 on a single product to create a drop shipping account. The best course of action is to inform the wholesaler of the problem and give $500 in advance as a credit line against orders. It assists you in meeting the minimum needed quantity, and you are not forced to place a huge order. You may now begin your search for the correct provider by distinguishing between a fake and a genuine wholesaler. You must assess which tactics are most effective for you:

✓ **Speak with your distributor.**

By far the simplest approach to discover a genuine wholesaler. If you know what commodities you want to view, just contact the company and enquire.

Instead, request a wholesale list. After that, you may both agree and make a phone call to check whether they accept drop shipping and how to set up an account.

✓ **Make use of Google Search**

This may appear to be self-evident, but bear the following in mind:
Because wholesalers aren't very excellent at marketing, you need to conduct a thorough search.
You may have to run hundreds of tests before you locate what you're looking for.
Normally, you won't be able to locate solid answers to your search until you've scrolled through the first ten pages of results. We don't have particularly up-to-date websites either, so don't pass judgement– A poorly designed, out-of-date website does not exclude them from providing you with a decent service. Because SEO is not extensively utilized by wholesalers, you will need to modify your search phrases.

The following are some or all of the six qualities of the top suppliers:

1. Professional personnel and a market focus

Suppliers should recruit professional sales representatives that are well-versed in the industry and can sell the items. You need to speak with someone who understands what they're talking about. 2. A dedicated support team.

Top-quality drop shipper's providers will assign you a specialized sales representative who will take care of you and help you with any difficulties or concerns that may occur. If you don't have a dedicated agent, you may have difficulties that take a long time to resolve and may need to call again and again to receive your answers. You will be able to create a more personal relationship with your delegate if you have a dedicated representative who is the only one with whom you speak.

3. Thorough technological research the majority of reputable suppliers have old websites, but a truly good firm would recognize and invest in technical benefits. These offer real-time inventory tracking, an extensive online database, configurable data costs, and online order history.

4. This may not seem like much, but it may take some time to ring in each order since it may need to be placed on the website. Orders should be placed through email. Accepting orders by email substantially speeds up the process.

5. If you reside in a large nation, such as the United States, it is simpler to hire a drop shipper that is centrally placed. This assures that you will send the majority of your purchases to your consumers within a few days. If your supplier is located on the coast, orders will take one or more weeks to complete and will cost extra due to shipping charges around the world.

6. Properly structured and successful suppliers with highly efficient people and solid systems that deliver a generally error-free service should be identified. Any other arrangement will wreak havoc on others.

The primary issue is that you can't evaluate your talents unless you use them, therefore it's advisable to place a modest test order with each of your favorite providers, even if it's time-consuming. You'll understand how it works, and you'll be able to determine: how effortlessly each organization manages the order procedure; how quickly they provide you with tracking information and bills;

When the order comes, it is of high quality. The majority of firms will pay for the order in one of two ways: Cards de credit when you begin your trip.

Identifying Wholesale Suppliers

Now that you know how to tell the difference between a scam and the actual thing, it's time to start looking for providers! You can employ a variety of techniques, some of which are more effective than others. The following approaches are presented in terms of efficacy and choice, beginning with our recommended methods:

Please contact the manufacturer.

This is my preferred method for swiftly finding genuine wholesale vendors. When you've decided on the product(s) you want to sell, contact the manufacturer and request a list of wholesale distributors. Then, send an email to these wholesalers to check whether they are drop shipping and to enquire about opening an account. Because most wholesalers offer items from a range of providers, this technique will help you to rapidly identify a variety of products within the area you are researching. You may simply locate the leading wholesalers in a market sector by making a few phone calls to the market's major producers.

Use Google to Search

Using Google Web to identify high-quality suppliers may appear to be simple, but there are a few guidelines to follow:
You Must Search Extensively–Because wholesalers are lousy at marketing and promotion, they are unlikely to appear at the top of search results for "Brand X wholesale suppliers." So, while a better website may indicate a better provider in some circumstances, many reputable wholesalers have cringe-worthy homepages. Don't be put off by the bad design.

Use a lot of modifiers–Because wholesalers do not utilize long SEOs to ensure that their websites are seen, you may need to use alternative search queries. Use phrases such as "distribution," "reseller," "bulk," "warehouse," and "manufacturer." Order from the Competitors if you can't find a supplier, you may always utilize the tried-and-true order-from-competition approach.

This is how it works:

Find a rival of the firm you believe is drop shipping and place a modest purchase with them. Once you've obtained the package, search for the return address label to determine who the original sender was. You may be able to contact a supplier at times. This is an approach that others have employed but that we haven't. And, if you haven't located a supplier using the other methods given above, there might be a solid reason for that (for example, the price is too low, there isn't enough product demand to justify a provider, etc.). So, keep the technique in mind, but don't put too much stock in it.

Participate at a trade exhibition - A trade show may help you connect with all of the key manufacturers and distributors in a specific industry. It is an excellent approach to gather all of your items and suppliers in one location to create contacts and do research. This only works if you've already identified your niche and/or product, which not everyone can. However, if you have the time and money to go, it's a great chance to meet a region's farmers and suppliers.

Registries - One of the most often asked concerns by budding ecommerce businesses is, "Do I have to pay for a supplier list?" A Supplier Directory is a listing of suppliers categorized by market, specialization, or product. Most directories use some sort of screening procedure to ensure that the vendors listed are real wholesalers. The majority are managed by for-profit businesses that demand a fee to use their database. While membership directories might be valuable, they are not required, especially when brainstorming ideas. If you already know the niche or product you want to offer, you should be able to identify the big suppliers in your industry with a little investigation using the tactics outlined above. Besides, you're unlikely to need to update the directory after your business is up and running unless you need to seek suppliers for new things.

Supplier directories, on the other hand, are a convenient method to rapidly identify and/or search a large selection of suppliers in one spot, and they are ideal for brainstorming ideas for product sales and niche entrance. If you are short on time and prepared to spend the money, they can be a useful tool. There are several supplier lists, and this guide's breadth extends beyond a full inspection. Alternatively, we've depicted some of the most well-known internet supplier directories. Please keep in mind that none of those folders is supported; we only provide you with some possibilities.

Worldwide Brands Quick Facts:

It was launched in 1999, and it now has millions of wholesalers and over ten million product prices. Worldwide Brands is one of the most well-known and oldest lifelong membership provider directories. It promotes that it only accepts suppliers that follow a set of rules to assure wholesalers' integrity and efficiency. In the past, we utilized the list to identify genuine wholesalers and product brainstorms, and we found the suggestions of legitimate wholesalers and product brainstorms to be useful.

Although some of the merchants with whom we work are not on the list, a huge number of lawful wholesalers are. Worldwide Brands is a solid choice if you want lifetime access to a premium directory and are willing to pay a higher one-time fee.

The Supplier Directory on Saleroom

This database has over 8,000 bulk purchasing and retail vendors, which appears to be quite similar to eBay and Amazon retailers. Over 8,000 bulk purchasing and retailing vendors are included in the Saleroom Supplier Directory. Although we have never used Saleroom to supply items, its yearly fee of 67 dollars is one of the most affordable for distributor directories and includes a 60-day money-back guarantee.
Saleroom is worth a look if you want to pay for an annual membership in a simple way, or if you only need to utilize a directory momentarily.
Rather than just listing suppliers, Doab's service is embedded into drop shippers (which will have only 165 providers), allowing you to make numerous warehouse orders through its unified interface. Quick facts about Doab: There are 165 suppliers.

More than 1.5 million goods Monthly cost is $60. Membership also includes a push-to-market tool that simplifies the eBay listing procedure. Because the centralized Doab system provides greater flexibility than other directories, the monthly fee of $60 is much more than the other tiers. If you're willing to pay a premium for usability and can locate the things you're looking for from their vendors, the Doab interface could be worth it. However, if you can discover credible suppliers on your own and don't mind dealing with them directly, you may save around $700 every year. If your market has only a few main suppliers, limiting the number of firms you must deal with, this may be the way to go.

Quick Stats for Wholesale Central:

In 1996, 1.400 suppliers established 740.000 products. Free of charge unlike many other directories, there is no price to look for Central wholesale sellers because the company pays suppliers a fee and also places advertisements on their websites. We also claim that all of our vendors have been reviewed and tested to guarantee that we are lawful and in compliance. There is no harm in browsing Wholesale Central's inventory, but you must be more discriminating. It's impossible to argue with the word "free." Many of the vendors we found appeared to be wholesalers selling to the public at wholesale pricing rather than manufacturers offering true wholesale prices. And, while we are certain that there are valid wholesale prospects, you may want to be a little more thorough in your due research.

You identify some reputable sources and are ready to go on till you contact the supplier–perfect! But, before you contact businesses, make sure you have all of your ducks in a row.

You must be legal—as previously said, most respectable wholesalers want proof that you are a legal business before you can register for an account. Because the majority of wholesalers only display their rates to approved customers, you must be legally licensed before you can see what type of deals you may receive. Finally, before approaching vendors, ensure that you are officially incorporated! If you merely want to ask a few simple questions ("Did you drop the ship?" "Do you carry brand X?"), no paperwork is required. However, don't expect to get started without a solid business setup. Later in this book, we'll go through how to set up your business.

Understand how you appear–Wholesalers are constantly inundated by consumers who ask questions, take their time, and never place an order. So, if you're thinking about starting a new business, keep in mind that many service providers won't assist you to get started. Most of them will gladly provide you with a drop shipping account. But don't ask for special pricing or waste hours on the phone before making a single transaction. It soon develops a negative reputation and harms your connection with the supplier.

You must be trustworthy if you need to make unique requests (for example, persuade a manufacturer to drop when it generally does not). Take care of your business plans ("We launch this website on 20 January") rather than using flimsy slogans ("I am thinking about starting a business perhaps someday"), and make sure you share some of your previous professional accomplishments, particularly in sales and marketing, that will help you with your new venture.

HOW TO LOCATE RELIABLE SUPPLIERS

Not all vendors are created equal. In the world of drop shipping, where the manufacturer is such an important element of the distribution cycle, dealing with top-tier companies is more important than ever. Many of the following six qualities are common among good suppliers: high-quality trained employees and knowledgeable suppliers with qualified sales representatives who know the industry and its product lines. Calling a representative with inquiries is helpful, especially if you are starting a shop in a field, you are unfamiliar with.

Drop shippers for results will assign a new sales agent to look after you and all your difficulties.

We've dealt with wholesalers that refuse to nominate particular reps because they don't like them. Problems take much longer to resolve, and we frequently have to nag individuals to do so. You must contact the firm in charge of resolving your issues.

Investigated technology–

While many reputable providers have outdated websites, dealing with a technology supplier who understands–and invests extensively in–the value of technology is usually a delight. Real-time inventory, a large online catalogue, customized data feeds, and online order history is all luxuries for online traders that may assist ease your operation. Orders may be placed by e-mail–this may appear to be a small issue, but it takes significantly longer to phone each order–or manually entered on the website.

Ideally located — if you live in a huge nation, such as the United States, centrally situated drop shippers can help you because deliveries can reach more than 90% of the country in 2-3 business days. When a supplier is on one of the coasts, it might take more than a week to ship orders around the world. You can confidently ensure speedier delivery times with central providers, saving you money on shipping expenses. Most manufacturers have skilled employees and strong systems in place, which results in quick and largely error-free delivery. Every fourth-order, others bite your hair and make you want to tear it out. The problem is that without employing it, it's difficult to determine how qualified a firm is in practice.

Although it will not provide you with a complete picture, completing a few modest test orders will provide you with a better sense of how a provider operates. How promptly the things are dispatched; how readily the details and invoice can be tracked when the item will be delivered; your selection of vendors and payment method.

The vast majority of suppliers accept one of two methods of payment:

1. The credit card.

Most vendors will need you to pay by credit card before you begin.

The following statements are correct: Once a profitable firm has been established, credit card payment is frequently the finest alternative. They are not only handy (no regular checks are required), but they also allow you to earn a lot of rewards points / frequent flyer miles. When you buy a product from a consumer on your website who has already paid for it, you may use your credit card to make a huge number of purchases without incurring any out-of-pocket charges.

2. Terms in Net

Another popular method of payment for suppliers is to invoice on "net terms." In essence, you have a certain number of days to pay the dealer for the products you have ordered. If you have been utilizing 'net 30'terminology, you must pay your vendor for the things you purchased within 30 days of delivery–by check or bank draw. Because they are lending you money, a supplier would generally want credit references before granting you net payment terms. This is a regular procedure, so don't be surprised if you pay on net terms when you have to provide any proof.

The last thing you want is to wind up with a bogus provider or one that does not follow your requirements. You end up with less money and a negative image among your clientele. It is less likely that you will choose a defective provider and set yourself up for success if you ensure that your supplier alternatives are selected and do not sign up for the first one you meet. You are now prepared to embark on a journey to locate the ideal supplier for your company plan and yourself, having learned how to select a reputable supplier, identify a fraudulent supplier, and put a stop to it. You will begin receiving orders from your clients after you have identified a vendor that will ship for you.

CHAPTER FOUR

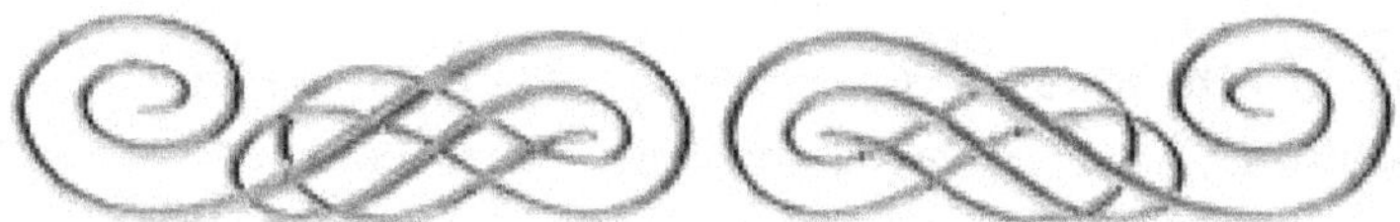

SELECTING THE BEST PRODUCTS TO DROPSHIP

C hoosing a niche with high-return items is the most difficult challenge for most new drop shipping companies. And it's understandable: it's arguably your most important decision, with long-term implications for business success or failure. The most typical blunder at this stage of the company is selecting a product based on personal interest or enthusiasm. This is an excellent method when the primary aim is not necessarily commercial success, but rather product interest. However, if your primary goal is to build a successful drop shipping platform, you should consider putting your interests in market research on hold, or at least make sure they satisfy the requirements given below.

You must accomplish one of the following to develop a successful e-commerce business: Produce your goods– You handle the delivery and are the item's exclusive source. It lowers competition and allows you to demand a higher price. If you wish to sell things, you must sell pre-existing products made by others, thus this is not an option.

⬚ Have access to exclusive pricing or distribution - If you can secure an exclusive commodities carrier deal–or access a distributor's exclusive pricing–you may sell online profitably without creating your goods. However, making these agreements may be complicated, since hundreds of other retailers have access to identical items and wholesale pricing.

⬚ Sell at the lowest possible price — if the lowest possible price is offered, the firm will most likely capture a sizable piece of the market.

What is the only question?

It's an unsustainable business model. If the only thing you have to offer is a cheap price, you will be trapped in a price war, and your money will be stolen. Fighting is typically a bad idea.

Amazon and other high-quality online retailers are interested in non-price keywords. The simplest approach to stand out and command a higher fee is to offer important information in addition to your services. Enterprises work to solve people's issues, and this is no different in the worlds of ecommerce and Drop shipping. The easiest way to build a thriving drop shipping business is to provide professional advice and recommendations in your industry.

Value

Simply add value to ecommerce! Isn't it just straightforward? Okay, indeed, the expression is easier said than done. Most niches and goods are more suited to this method than others. You should search for several essential elements that will make it much easier to add value to instructional content.

Product images of high quality

You must guarantee that customers are familiar with the goods and that high-quality product images continue to be obtained. Burst is a website where you may get free product photographs. It also contains some business suggestions for starting and running your shop. The more aspects a product need to perform effectively, the more likely users are to seek solutions on the internet. What could be a more difficult investment? Should you buy a new office chair or a home security surveillance system that requires many cameras, intricate wires, and a recorder? The larger the product's requirements and the greater the diversity of its components, the greater the chance to provide value by advising consumers on comparable items. Specific Customized and configurable things are perfect for providing value through content in the same vein.

You know instinctively how to choose the ideal set of hot water solar panels for your situation, or what type of Wi-Fi dog collar system is perfect for your yard. A more straightforward method to offer value is to provide precise advice on what sorts of items are most suited for specific surroundings and clients.

Professional setup or installation is required — Expert guidance is simple to offer for goods that are difficult to mount, assemble, and configure. Consider the above-mentioned security camera equipment. Assume the camera site provided a thorough 50-page installation guide that also addressed the most frequent problems individuals make when installing their systems. If you believe the guide would save you time and hassle, it would be a good idea to purchase it on this page, even if it is less expensive elsewhere.

The guidelines provide significant value to store owners while costing nothing to produce.

How to provide value: There are several methods to bring value to difficult and perplexing niches, including

▢ Creating detailed buyer guides Investing in comprehensive product descriptions and listings
▢ The development of instructional films (as previously described) to demonstrate how the product works, among other things.

The correct demographics might be a huge help to your company. Such clients are more likely to make excellent use of their time:

Enthusiasts – These are people who are passionate about their hobbies and spend a lot of money on equipment, training, and supplies. Most dedicated mountain bikers have bikes that are more expensive than their automobiles, while fishermen can spend a lot on their boats. You may perform extremely well if you target the correct segment of hobbyists and communicate well with enthusiasts and their requirements.

Corporate clients are frequently more cost-conscious than individual customers, but they nearly always purchase in bigger numbers. Once you've established a relationship and gained their trust, you've opened the door to a long-term, very profitable partnership. Attempt to market things that reach both individual customers and corporations as much as feasible. Repeat Purchasers – The recurring revenue is fairly satisfactory. If you sell things that are readily available and/or must be purchased regularly, you will swiftly expand by building a devoted customer base that frequently returns to buy. Other factors to consider when purchasing goods

The best pricing – Please test the pricing point of your pre-sale service. Many consumers are at ease ordering a $200 order online without speaking with anyone on the phone. But what about an unknown object priced at $1,500? Most people would prefer to talk with a salesperson before making such a large purchase, both to check that the item fits correctly and to ensure that the company is authentic. If you want to offer low-cost things, be sure your gadgets can provide individualized support. Before you offer the service, you must also ensure that the margins are sufficient to support it. Without a solid pre-sale's assistance, the $30 to $250 price range is frequently a good location to optimize income.

MAP Pricing — many manufacturers are permitted to price their goods at or above the minimum agreed-upon price (MADP). This pricing plan serves to prevent price wars, which are common – especially for commodities that are readily moved down – and ensures that merchants may earn a healthy profit by transporting a supplier's products. It is a huge benefit if you can identify a product niche where manufacturers may price MAP, especially if you want to establish a worthwhile and informative site. You can compete on the strength of your website, with pricing that is the same across all rivals, and you won't have to worry about losing business to less reputable but less costly competitors.

Marketing potential – Not three months later, when you find that client acquisition is a nightmare, you must consider how you will advertise a firm before it is started. Can you think of a variety of strategies to advertise your business, such as publishing articles, promoting products, or reaching out to active online groups with the items you sell? If not, perhaps you should rethink.

Selling a product with several accessories is an excellent approach to increase total profit.

Several attachments – Lower-priced accessories, on average, have much larger margins than higher-priced goods. While a mobile phone retailer may only get a 5% profit on a new smartphone, it will almost surely achieve a 100 or 200 per cent margin in that situation.

They are also more sensitive to the price of large-scale manufacturing and less concerned with the price of smaller items as consumers. To utilize the example above, you will most likely go searching for an expensive smartphone at the best price. But are you going to contact me to get the greatest deal on a \$20-\$30 case? Maybe not. You'll most likely purchase it from the same store where you purchased the phone.

Low sales–We hope you are now convinced that investing in a high-quality educational platform will pay you handsomely. However, if the things you offer vary every year, it will quickly become a mountain of labor to maintain the platform. Look for goods that aren't updated with new models every year. And your time and money will be better spent if you use a good platform.

Difficult to localize - As long as you are not too particular, selling a local product that is hard to obtain boosts your chances of success. Some folks would just go to the hardware shop if they needed a garden rake or a sprinkler. But where would you go to get a mediaeval knight's garb or falcon training gear? You'd probably go to Google and continue.

Smaller is typically preferable – Selling large, high-priced equipment might be difficult in a world when everyone expects free shipping. The smaller the goods, the easier it is to distribute to your clients at a low cost.

Choosing a lucrative niche is difficult and requires you to consider several variables. Such recommendations will provide you with a decent notion of the type of things that will be supplied. Measuring competition without demand is pointless if your niche meets all of the criteria listed above. You'll struggle to make money if no one wants your stuff! It is far simpler to fulfil current demand than it is to try to manufacture it, as the adage goes.

Fortunately, there are various online tools available to calculate commodity or market demand, the most well-known and widely used of which is the Google Keyword Tool. The greatest approach to gauge online demand for an item is to check how many people are searching for it on a search engine like Google. Fortunately, Google makes this search traffic public via its keyword tool. Simply enter a phrase or term, and the tool will tell you how many people search for it each month.

There are whole training programmers dedicated to the use of the keyword tool, and we will not be able to cover it all in this book. However, if you follow these three suggestions, you will be on the right route to getting the most out of the programmer.

The Match Type - App lets you select broad groups of terms or exact matches while keeping track of search volumes. Except for very excellent reasons, you should pick the exact match option. This will provide you with a far more thorough view of search volume.

Search location- Be sure to consider the difference between local and worldwide search volume (in your nation or area). If you only sell in the United States, you should focus on local search rates and disregard national results because this is where the majority of your clients are.

Long-Tail Variations– It is straightforward to repair the little, one- or two-word search keywords that are often used. In reality, the majority of your search engine traffic is made up of lengthier, more complex, and lower frequency search inquiries. Long-distance searches are frequently referred to by such lengthier and more complex search terms.

Consider this while looking at possible markets and successful niches. If a search phrase contains multiple versions that are regularly searched, it is a positive indication that demand is fairly broad, with a wide range of variety and value. When, on the other hand, search queries and related volumes drop fast after the first few high-level phrases, there is likely less long-distance traffic.

Google Trends

The keyword tool is good for raw search data, but Google Trends is better for in-depth research. The tool will offer you information that the keyword tool does not, such as The Evolution of Search Volume: Hopefully, you wish to extend the market into which you are venturing, and patterns will indicate this. You may monitor the change in search volume for any search term over time. The number of searches has increased dramatically in recent years.

Images in high quality - You may also get a visual representation of the most popular related searches and which questions are becoming the most popular. As marketing and SEO methods evolve, it might be beneficial to concentrate on certain phrases. According to the data below, AT&T, Verizon, and Samsung search inquiries continue to show the most increase in the smartphone market: the geographic concentration: Another important feature is the ability to discover where people are looking for a phrase right now. This might assist you in determining the most oriented target client base. Maps can assist you to identify, for example, that the majority of your clients originate from the North of the United States, Alaska, and Hawaii. When deciding between different suppliers, this information may allow you to work with someone who is nearest to the majority of your clients.

Seasonality knowing a market's seasonality is vital when the demand for a product varies substantially throughout the year. Because the keyword tool only provides monthly data, you may draw incorrect conclusions if you evaluate search levels at the wrong time of year.

In our earlier example, we can observe that the search keyword for high demand seasons in the summer months. If you compute demand in the summer as if it is constant all year, you will dramatically exaggerate the magnitude of demand: you will want to invest time understanding the subtleties of market search volume for any product that you are serious about. By taking into account search rates, regional distribution, high levels of searching behaviors, and seasonal circumstances, the Google Trend tool can help you avoid costly mistakes and maximize your marketing efforts.

Competition Evaluation

Market analyses on a potential market might be difficult. If there is too much competition, it will be tough to increase traffic and compete with established competitors. Too little rivalry might result in a narrow market, limiting your ability to grow significantly. Many shops utilize paid advertising, but the majority rely largely on free visitors from search engines to generate a profit. In this regard, the easiest way to gauge overall competitiveness in a sector is to conduct a Google search for organically identified (that is, unannounced) Websites on the first page for a certain topic. To obtain a fair quantity of traffic, you must successfully compete with the sites on Google's first page, i.e. outrank.

Google's Linking Domains ranking algorithm is inextricably linked. The more connections a website has in search results, the better. Understanding how many links connect to a website offers you an indication of how much work you will have to put in (in earning and establishing links to your website) to outperform your competitor. There are hundreds of SEO measures, but one, in particular, is important for determining the strength of a site's ranking: the number of unique sites linking to it. This statistic, also known as "connected root domains" or "one-way relation domains," reflects the number of distinct domains (e.g., independent sources) linked to a site after excluding duplicate connections from a domain.

To further comprehend this notion, consider relationships such as personal referrals. If your closest buddy comes to you and suggests a restaurant, you can remember that name; if he receives recommendations every day (let's say, a total of seven suggestions) and raves about it for a week, you will undoubtedly want to dine at that place. Even his enthusiasm, though, would not be nearly as exciting as if seven unconnected friends all strongly praised the restaurant. We will place significantly greater trust in their opinions because they come from independent sources.

When links to a website are analyzed, the same thing happens. A domain that often connects to a site, however, is a "private" suggestion, and traditional SEO measurements, such as "the total number of links," might provide an imperfect image when gauging site strength. Looking at the number of unique connection domains in the search results, on the other hand, will show you how tough it is to compete with the competition. Google highlights the relationship between particular domains, and you should as well.

Using an Open Web Explorer tool is the easiest method to accomplish this. Samos's Open Site Explorer provides a variety of important SEO metrics and data. For full capability, you will need to purchase a premium membership, however, you can acquire the metric you want–"Connection root domains"–as provided by the app for free.

Look at the Google search results for the first few pages (Google #1 and #2) and the last site rankings on the main page (Google #10). This provides you with a sense of how much work is required to get this not just to #1, but also to the first search result page. To illustrate how difficult, it is to identify the domain, the great majority of searches end up clicking the top 10 results on Google.

Here is a quick cheat sheet to help you understand how many distinct domains are linked. (These are only basic recommendations, but they should help you understand the data.) 0 to 50 Connect root domains: the most profitable marketplaces are likely to be at the bottom. Many high-quality websites with targeted marketing and SEO study should be able to gain 50 connected domains within a year.

Connecting 50-250 Root Domains: This is a more realistic price range for premium sites in recognized specialized markets. It will take several years to build a backlink profile in this industry, but it is doable. A competitive environment with this type frequently provides the finest job-to-reward ratio for solo drop shippers or extremely small teams.

- 250+ Root Domains for Linking: If you are a highly skilled marketer or SEO ninja, it will take time and effort to develop more than 250 unique relationships. It isn't always an assassin–just be prepared to compete. When determining a site's grade, Google considers more than simply the number of links it has. It also considers the essence of these relationships. As a result, a connection to five Mike's Marshmallow Blog followers will not be as valuable as a similar link from the New York Times.

- PageRank is a Google metric that is used to determine the authority of a website. This isn't the end of SEO analytics, but it's a quick method to determine how significant a Google page thinks it is. The PageRank homepages of top-ranking sites, such as different connection sites, will give you an idea of how competitive a market is. A browser plugin, such as Firefox Search Status, is the best way to check PageRank. You may also manually verify web pages with programmers like this one.

Here's a quick method to interpret PageRank values for a website's homepage:

- PageRank 1 to 2: A modest number of authorities. PageRank may imply a very small market for the top homepages in this category.

- PageRank 3 to 4: This is a far more frequent range for high-ranking sites in competitive specialized sectors; it is not simple to attain, but it is not impossible. Individual shippers often find the finest range of work-for-reward opportunities in markets in this category.

- PageRank 4–5: a rather high degree of authority. To attain this level, you will need multiple connections from reputable, authoritative sources, in addition to a range of other links.

⬚ PageRank 6+: You're in good hands with the sales staff and SEO, okay? Because you will require them to succeed in a market with such sites.

Qualitative measures that take into account hard information, such as specific connected domains and PageRank, may help in determining how difficult it is for outdoor competitors. However, it is also critical to investigate a few qualitative factors that influence site efficiency and usability.

⬚ Are they nice and inviting, or are they ancient and out of date?

⬚ Are the pages well-organized and simple to use, or is the search box difficult to locate?

Do they give thorough product listings and high-quality details, or do you have to crack the company's blurry images?

How frequently would you buy from these websites? If you are blown away by a company's top positions, it will be difficult to differentiate yourself, and you may want to choose another firm. Regardless, whether there is a lot of room for improvement or an opportunity to add value, this is a fantastic indicator.

Customer loyalty and site credibility–

⬚ Even though an outdated design and website are apparent, an online firm might have a great reputation built on years of client service. In contrast, even the most attractively designed platform may have a bad reputation for poor customer service. It might be challenging to evaluate a book by its cover.

⬚ Consult a well-known Business brand to determine whether a firm has a history of client complaints. You should also conduct a web search to discover what others are saying on social media, forums, and online communities. A superior store can be created if the top competitors in quality and satisfaction are lax.

Take notice of the search results.

It is critical to understand that Google adjusts the search results based on your location, browsing history, and other criteria. We need accurate data while assessing a sector so that we may comprehend the true competitive environment. Furthermore, you must have access to the search results that your US clients will view, as these are the areas in which you will compete if you live outside of the US but intend to sell to US consumers.

There are two approaches to dealing with these issues:

Search incognito: If you use Chrome as your browser, you may search for the 'Incognito' app. Every custom setting or browsing history is removed in this mode, giving you an unbiased picture of how the sites truly rank. You may launch an Incognito browsing session by selecting 'File New Incognito Window' or by hitting 'New Incognito Window.' Other web browsers have similar hidden search settings that erase your browsing history.

Country-forcing: Specific results: add a short piece of text to the end of the URL on a Google results page to obtain country-specific results if you want the results that display in a nation other than your own.

For example, if you were in the United Kingdom but wanted search results from searches in the United States, you would add the "& gal= us" parameter to the end of the URL on the search results page. Similarly, if you were in the US and desired UK performance, you should add "& gal= UK" at the end of the URL.

One final concern I understand drop shippers have been being able to answer the question, "How can I be confident my niche will work?" You can't, that's for sure! While the techniques and advice in this chapter will greatly improve your chances and help you make educated decisions, there is no guarantee that you will succeed in a company unless you start one. We began several enterprises, some of which flourished and others of which failed, and we were always skeptical at the outset. This is part of the fear that comes with starting a business and venturing into the unknown. What distinguishes entrepreneurs from mere dreamers is a desire to move forward and give it their all despite the uncertainty.

So, learn, investigate, and amass as much knowledge as you can. But then, despite your reservations and reservations, choose the finest decision. You will not begin if you wait for "the ideal market" to resolve all of the issues.

CHAPITRE FIVE

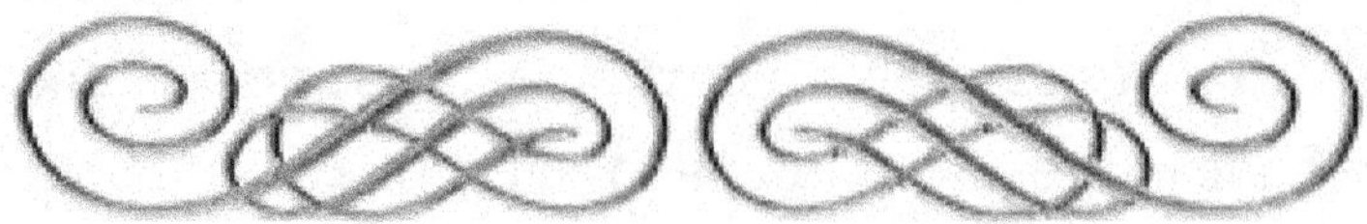

GETTING YOUR COMPANY STARTED

ou must understand the principles of drop shipping before you contemplate beginning your own business. If you're serious about starting a new business, you should think about taking the next steps before you launch. Some are required from the start, while others are optional, but tackling them will save you time and headaches down the road. Building a profitable drop shipping business, like any other, necessitates a significant investment and a long-term vision. If you expect to make a six-figure salary from a part-time job in six weeks, you will be disappointed. You are considerably less likely to be dissatisfied and resign if you approach the company with realistic estimates of necessary investment and profitability. When launching a drop shipping business, you must invest extensively in one of two currencies: time or money.

Investing Time

Bootstrapping time and equity investment for developing your business is encouraged, especially for entrepreneurs who have done a few drop shipping enterprises in the past. You support this philosophy of spending big quantities of money for a variety of reasons: you understand how the business operates from the inside out, which is critical to dealing with people as the firm develops and expands. You are well-versed in your clients' and competitors' businesses, allowing you to make more informed decisions. It may be more difficult, but you can surely begin drop shipping even if you already work 9 to 5 given you set the necessary customer service and delivery timings for your consumers. When you're finished, you can transition into full-time cash flow and efficiency work for your company. Every firm and contractor is unique, but within 12 months, a $1,000-$2,000 monthly revenue stream that operates between 10-15 hours per week to build the company may be produced.

If you have the option to work full-time in your business, it is the ideal way to enhance your productivity and performance. It is especially beneficial to concentrate all of your marketing efforts in the early stages when it is critical to developing momentum. Based on our experience, it would typically take at least 12 months of full-time work to replace an average full-time wage of $50,000 and significantly emphasize the marketing of a drop shipping firm.

It may appear like you are putting in a lot of effort for a minimal reward, but keep these two points in mind: Once your shipping firm is up and going, it will most likely take far less time to sustain than 40-hour-per-week employment. Given the drop shipping model's adaptability and scalability, a large portion of your investment will be repaid. When you construct a company, you generate more than simply an income stream; you create an asset that you may sell in the future. Take into account the worth of the equities you invest in as well as the cash flow generated to your genuine return.

Investing money

A large quantity of money can be used to establish and expand an investing firm, but we advise against it. We tested both ways to grow a firm (bootstrapping vs. outsourcing) and found the most success in the trenches. In the early phases, someone must spend actively in the development of establishing the firm from the ground up. You are at the whim of pricey programmers, developers, and advertising that readily swallow any revenues you generate without understanding how your firm runs at every step. You don't have to do everything alone, but we highly advise that you be the major driving force at the start of your firm.

However, to establish and manage your firm, you will need a little financial buffer in the $1,000 level. This is adequate for small running expenditures (such as web hosting and suppliers), and any incorporation fees that we discuss below can be paid.

Please keep in mind that the information on the company structure and EIN (employer identification number) is exclusive to US businesses and will not apply to organizations in other countries. See the notes at the end of this chapter for information about integrating a US-based corporation from outside the US.

When you take your firm seriously, you'll want to establish a legal corporate organization. We are not attorneys and cannot provide legal advice, however, we can offer you an outline of three regularly used business structures: Ownership is sufficient, but it does not protect personal culpability. This is the simplest company structure to implement. As a result, your assets may also be in danger if you're company-issued. The reporting criteria are modest, and you just record your company revenue on your taxes. Other federal or state-owned corporation registrations are not necessary.

Limited Liability Firm (LLC) – The LLC provides better security for your assets by forming your company as a separate legal entity. While the defense of responsibility is not dumb, it provides greater protection than exclusive ownership. You may be required to complete extra filing requirements and pay both incorporation and ongoing costs.

C – Corporation – Most big organizations are structured to give the best level of liability protection when carried out correctly as Corporations. These may be more difficult to implement and liable to double taxation since sales are not transmitted directly to shareholders.

So, which shape should you go with? Also, because we are not attorneys, we strongly advise you to consult with one before making any incorporation choices. Many small businesses decide to form a single corporation or an LLC. We also employed an LLC for all of our drop shipping businesses since we think that it provides the greatest insurance in terms of liability protection, the flexibility of personal funding, and expenses.

Requesting an EIN Number

Every organization is required by the IRS to obtain an EIN, which is your company's Social Security number. You'll need this number to submit your taxes, apply for wholesale accounts, create a bank account, and conduct a variety of other things for your business. Fortunately, acquiring an EIN code is simple and cost-free. An EIN may be obtained quickly and easily online.

Get your money in order.

Businessmen frequently make the mistake of combining their personal and corporate finances when launching a new venture. It creates confusion, complicates bookkeeping, can add to the personal impression of client responsibility, and is a major red flag for the IRS if you are ever audited. You'll want to keep your business and personal funds as separate as feasible. The best approach to achieve this is to gain access to the company's new accounts. You'll want to start a new one: A corporate checking account should handle all of your company's money. It should deposit and subtract all expenditures in favor of all business revenue.

Accounting will become simpler and safer as a result of this.

- ▢ PayPal Account–If you wish to approve PayPal payments for your business, you will need to establish a separate account (which you certainly do).
- ▢ Credit Card–You should have a company credit card that is exclusively used to purchase firms and stock exchanges. With the correct rewards card, if you buy a lot of things from stores, you may build up some substantial rewards. We identify the best travel rewards programmer for Capital One and Fidelity. Visa / American Express is the greatest cash-back programmer for the deal.

You will only have to collect sales tax if both of the following conditions are met: **THE STATE IN WHICH YOU WORK FROM THE SALES TAX** AND An order is placed by someone residing in your nation for all orders placed by residents of other states–even if they implement their own sales tax–they will not have to pay any cost. There is a significant likelihood that these restrictions may be amended in the coming years, but for the time being, tax legislation is extremely beneficial to small internet shops.

If your state levies a sales tax, be prepared to collect a small proportion of purchases from clients in your home nation. To register as a retailer, you must contact the Commerce Department in your state to determine how frequently you must apply the tax that you collect. Many cities and municipalities enable businesses to get a business license, which must be renewed regularly. This criterion may change for drop shipping firms, although many of them are likely to be run from home offices. You should study local rules and regulations to determine what is necessary.

Incorporating

Drop shippers and US consumers might be tough to find outside the United States, as overseas sellers can incorporate a firm within the United States. The trader must go to the United States to complete the proper papers, have a trustworthy business partner in the United States who can act on his behalf, or engage an agency to set up anything. You can get started with the materials listed below, but we highly advise you to consult a legal professional before making any decisions.

For most people, eBay is a well-known website since it is the world's largest physical trade network. Here are some reasons why you might want to reconsider–or discontinue–shipping on eBay: eBay Pros of Selling - It is simple to get started. With eBay, you can rapidly delve into your wholesale products and start listing them. Make an account, add a list, and you're ready to go. Link to a huge audience-You has a connection to the numerous online clients that frequent the auction behemoth on the eBay list.

- Millions of people will view your ads, and a pretty vigorous and aggressive competition will assist to guarantee that your things are priced reasonably.
- Less Advertising-Because the principal eBay site may be piggybacked, you don't need to worry about advertising, SEO, or traffic fees. It saves you time because one of the most difficult aspects of running a drop shipping business is promoting it.
- The biggest downside of eBay Listing Costs-eBay is the fees you'll have to pay. The most striking is the performance incentive, which may be up to 10% or more of the selling prices of your things. In the drop shipping market, where margins are already thin, this will take a big portion of your earnings.
- Constant auditing and re-listing-Because eBay is an auction-format marketplace, you must continually monitor and re-list anything you wish to sell. Most solutions make this procedure easier, but displaying a static product on your ecommerce website is not yet as straightforward.
- Can't personalize your sales platform – It's tough to construct a good value-added page for your products that fits eBay templates.
- No long-term consumer connection–You may have a few repeat customers on eBay, but the vast majority of them will never buy from you again. The goodwill you get from providing outstanding service is likely to be lost. The marketplace system is designed to serve itself. You don't want to focus on the merchants; instead, you want to focus on the items. You'll

be severely restricted in how you contact clients, market yourself, design your business, and so on.

▢ When you construct a store with clients and customers, you are not creating an asset; rather, you are creating a real value firm that you can sell to someone else. You do not establish a permanent mark or online property with the monetary worth that you may sell on eBay in the future.

Amazon Drop shipping

Though Amazon stores and sells certain things, many of the products mentioned are offered to third-party merchants via the Amazon marketplace.
Unlike eBay, Amazon attempts to make it easy to sell and address difficulties.

The advantages of selling on Amazon are comparable to those of eBay: you get quick access to a large audience and don't have to worry about advertising or SEO. Amazon also has its fulfilment facilities (Amazon Fulfillment), which allow you to add your things to your delivered items without having to bother with packaging, shipping, and warehousing.

The downsides of the Amazon listing fee–

As with eBay, you must pay a rather high fee to gain access to this vast buyer's network. Amazon's commission rates vary depending on the goods; however, they often range between 10% and 15%.
Furthermore, a big portion of your income is derived from jobs with rather low drop shipping margins.

▢ Access to sales data—one danger of using the Amazon website is that Amazon will be able to access all of your sales information, from the goods you sell to the overall sales. Amazon has been accused of using this data to locate large selling opportunities and to improve its market position.

▢ There is no long-term relationship with consumers– You, like eBay, are skeptical of your ability to establish long-term client connections. Amazon exists to assist itself, and it is in its best interests to focus on the items rather than the sellers. Be prepared to firmly limit yourself to branding, displaying items, and connecting with your clientele.

▢ There will be no customization–as with eBay, you will be quite close in terms of setting. All you have control over is branding, user interface, marketing, and everything else. Setting up your online store is an option to sell things on third-party platforms like Amazon and eBay. This is the most critical approach for establishing a successful drop shipping service.

You may create a shopping experience with your online store to sell your products and, most importantly, give value to your clients. The advantages of having extra capacity at your store.

You may change the style and feel as well as build unique, customizable product pages to inform your consumers about the best items.

Design is straightforward.

It is simple to create your e-commerce site, especially with systems like Shopify. Simply choose a shop template from hundreds of options, personalize your products, add your things, connect a payment gateway, and you're ready to go.

You may run and run in one day, depending on the sort of internet business you're looking for.

Prepared for App

Selling on eBay and Amazon might be a chore. If you opt to construct your online store with a reputable e-commerce provider, your site will most likely be open, making your iPad or mobile phone appear excellent. This is becoming increasingly significant in today's world since roughly 30% of internet sales are performed via mobile phones that generate a genuine brand–you may construct a long-standing business with a unique presence, professional expertise, and repeat clients. Most essential, you must establish an equity fund. It is considerably easier to sell a firm developed around a distinct website. The disadvantages of selling on your website are you can generate traffic using your website through marketing, SEO, and paid to advertise; however, there are additional costs involved–whether you invest in money or time–and you must be prepared to invest in a long-term campaign to promote your new store.

CHAPTER SIX

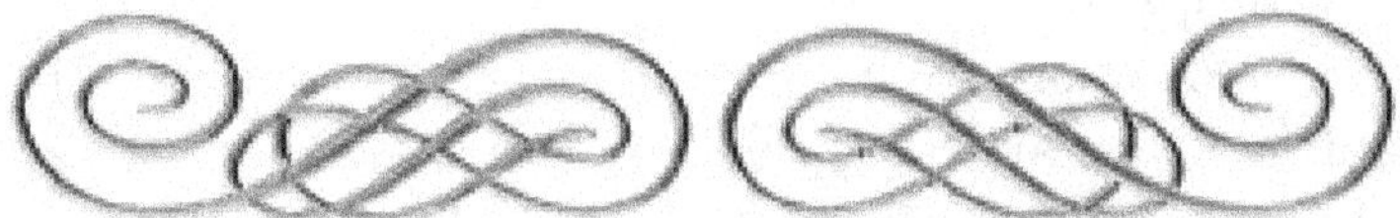

RUNNING A DROPSHIPPING COMPANY

I f you have never run a drop shipping firm, you may avoid weeks of wasted time and anguish by reading this chapter. Many of these all-encompassing ideas are founded on two essential principles:

1. **Also, keep in mind that the convenience of messy–**drop shipping comes at a cost, and the existence of an unknown third party in each transaction frequently complicates issues. Distribution concerns will have to be addressed, from failed orders to outsourced products.

If you consider this ahead of time, you are less likely to give up due to irritation.

2. **Use the KISS attitude** — With the KISS approach, keep things basic and quick – this will help you with the drop shipping model. Because of the inherent complexity of various suppliers and shipments from different locations, etc., it is easy to feel that you require a system to correctly monitor your expenses and inventories. But if you tried, you'd probably go insane, spend thousands on bespoke manufacture, and never open a store. Emphasizing the simplest solutions to execute, even if they aren't "complete," is typically the best option–especially when you're just getting started. In light of these two concepts, let's look at how to arrange the firm operationally to ensure that everything runs as smoothly as possible. Even large suppliers make mistakes when placing an order, and you may have received incorrect deliveries from time to time. And what if your supplier provides the wrong item or nothing at all?

Own the fault-You should never, ever blame your drop shipper for a mistake. It just makes you feel disoriented and inexperienced. The consumer is unaware that a drop shipper exists.

Instead, you must own the problem, apologies, and inform the consumer of your plans to rectify it.

- Make it up to them–depending on the severity of the fault, you may want to proactively provide the consumer with a mistake. This might be a refund of the delivery price (our personal preference) or an upgrade if the consumer requires a new item to be delivered. You may have to accept responsibility for the error, but it doesn't imply you have to pay for it!

Any competent provider would pay to correct their errors, such as repaying return merchandise for shipping charges. However, it is unlikely that it will pay for any freebies or upgrades that you have offered to the customer. We must be considered as public relations and brand development expenses. Even the finest suppliers make mistakes from time to time, so pay careful attention to a provider that frequently botches and fails to fulfil orders accurately. Your reputation will suffer if you can (unlikely) replace the manufacturer.

- If this is the case, you should probably start looking for another provider. The majority of experienced horsepower firms think that the most difficult task for a horsepower company is managing inventory status across numerous vendors. If you do this incorrectly, you will repeatedly alert clients that their item is out of stock–not a good approach to re-attract loyal brand lovers.

Proper inventory management–and limiting the number of stock products you offer–by your providers is a difficult procedure. Web-based systems such as Ordure and eCommHub can assist with stock syncs. This is an excellent alternative since providers have real-time data streams, but they do not always have them. The following are some of the greatest stock management tactics for reducing the number of production stocks you sell: access to numerous distributors–having access to many suppliers may be a major benefit. Why? Why? For what purpose? What? Having many suppliers with varying stocks is the greatest method to enhance the order execution ratio.

When supplier A does not have any items in stock, supplier B has a strong opportunity. Furthermore, the product is dangerous because it is dependent on a single provider as its sole source. If you refuse to work with what is available, raise rates, or abandon the firm, you will damage the future of your company. There will always be two vendors that provide the same product, but both will typically stock the best-selling items because they work in the same industry or sector, which is what you are most concerned about.

Select your things wisely— try to sell largely things from both vendors that you are familiar with. As a result, you have two fulfilment alternatives.

Take Advantage of Generics–

Even if they do not have the same thing, two suppliers will have nearly equivalent interchangeable products. It specifically refers to minor attachments and add-ons. When two commodities are shown to be nearly identical, please provide a generic product description that will allow you to fulfil either supplier's order. List the model numbers of the two providers in the model's region. The order invoice can then be forwarded to either supplier without alteration. A word of caution: you must use caution in this situation. - The market will include well-known brands (such as Nike and Bose) that you should NEVER replace.

Check for item availability–Just because a drop shipper has an item on its website does not indicate the item is in stock regularly. It is a good idea to discuss the pricing of the things you intend to sell with your sales representative. Are these items in stock 90% of the time or more? Or does the drop shipper keep a few in touch and frequently struggle to repurchase the supplier's sample? You'll want to cease storing this kind of item.

Managing Out-of-Stock Orders

Regardless of how well you prepare, you will have to dispute your order at some point. You are unable to carry out your request. Allow a free upgrade to a comparable product instead of informing the buyer that the item is out of stock. The consumer is really happy, and you may keep the connection going.

It's fine if you can't earn money on orders. You would not have made any money if your client's order was cancelled.

Numerous providers provide the benefits we highlighted here: It enhances the possibility that goods will be in stock, allows geographic flexibility for faster delivery times, and avoids you from relying on a single supplier to supply your products. But, with so many suppliers to select from, how do you know which one to go with?

There are numerous options to consider: All orders should be routed to a certain supplier– If you have one of the best suppliers with whom you can work (excellent service, a large selection, etc.), you may easily forward all orders to that provider by default. This is very easy to implement since you just add your supplier's email address as a recipient for all new order confirmations and automate the entire process. If you utilize this method, the majority of the items you offer will most likely be processed by your chosen manufacturer.

Otherwise, you'll frequently have to deal with requests for re-routing that it can't handle.

Orders may be routed depending on their location if you employ numerous suppliers to supply the bulk of your items. This allows you to rapidly transmit the order to the supplier closest to your client. This not only speeds up distribution to your client but also saves money on shipping expenses.

Route orders depending on availability–

When you have a huge inventory distributed across numerous suppliers, you may have to send each order on which the shipper stocks the item. If you, do it manually, you may use a tool like eCommHub (www.ecommhub.com) to automate it if your suppliers give the data streams.

Route orders based on price–

It sounds fantastic in principle, but deciding which source is the lowest might be difficult if another company has a considerably lower price. Any automated system will take future cost reductions, real-time shipping rates, and supplier prices into consideration. As a result, while not impossible, implementing a sophisticated automated system might be challenging. Even if your orders are not completed at a price, the suppliers should compete against each other to attain the best feasible pricing as the firm expands. Consider not starting too soon–if you're seeking possibilities to be handled as a rookie, the merchants may be annoying. All four ways have been tried, and no "right" method has been discovered. It is determined by your company, suppliers, and personal preferences. Fraud and security Keeping Credit Card Information

Keep your clients' credit card information on file to make reordering easier and maybe enhance sales. However, if you manage your website, security issues and liabilities are usually not worth it. To keep your credit card information secure, you must follow all PCI (Payment Card Industry) compliance rules and security assessments. This is a costly and complicated exercise, especially for non-technical traders. In addition, if your account is compromised or damaged, you may be held accountable for the contents of your wallet.

The ideal option is to not save the credit card information of the clients. Rather than security audits, concentrate your resources on marketing and customer service.

Fortunately, if you utilize a host platform like Shopify, you won't have to worry about any of that. However, if you are using a self-hosted cart, be sure that the "store card information" feature is disabled in your settings panel.

Handling bogus orders

The possibility of fraudulent orders might be alarming, but with a little common sense and prudence, you can avoid the great majority of losses due to fraud. The most popular and extensively used approach for combating fraud is the AVS or Address Verification System. Customers must enter their credit card addresses in their files to authorize the transaction after the AVS function is deactivated. This helps to prevent fraudsters from successfully dealing electronically using only the credit card number. Fraud is uncommon for purchases that adhere to the AVS requirement and are delivered to the customer's billing addresses.

The great majority of fraudulent ecommerce orders occur when the billing and distribution addresses vary. In such circumstances, the thief must put the card owner's address as the billing address and a distinct mailing address. Unfortunately, if you don't allow clients to send orders to addresses other than the billing address, you'll miss a lot of valid orders. However, you run the risk of accepting fake requests, for which you may be charged. In the event of fraud, the credit card company will require you to pay the charge if you send an order to an address different from the cardholders.

Fortunately, fraudsters prefer to follow patterns, making it easier to discover unlawful orders before they ship. These are not separate indicators of a fake order, but if you observe two or three of them, you can investigate:

Similar billing and shipping — once again, almost 95 per cent of all fraudulent orders are charged and delivered differently.

- Different names–Different names may be a red flag for fraudulent billing and shipping address purchases.

- Extraordinary e-mail addresses–Many individuals have e-mail addresses that contain portions of their names to link the aspect of the e-mail address to the corporate name. If you notice an address like dfssdfsdf@gmail.com, it is a false address and a symptom of fraud; there is a strong probability.

- Expedited shipping–Because they charge everything on someone else's account, fraudsters frequently want the quickest and most costly mode of distribution. It also shortens the time it takes to collect the thing before sending it.

Simply pick up your phone if you come across an order that you suspect is fake. Fraudsters seldom place an order for their phone number. If the order is genuine, you will normally have a 30-second discussion with someone who will explain everything. Otherwise, you'll get a dead number or someone who has no idea a 25-foot boat will be transported overnight. To prevent costs or issues, you should cancel the order and issue a refund at that moment.

If a consumer calls a bank or credit card provider to dispute a cost you charged, you will receive a "chargeback." The payment processor will take the disputed cost from your account automatically and ask you to confirm that the products or services have been dispatched to your client. If you are unable to produce documentation, you will forfeit the balance and be charged a $25 chargeback processing fee. You may lose your vendor account if you receive too many refunds in contrast to the number of orders you manage. Fraud is probably the most common reason for payback, but it can also be because customers have forgotten about your organization, forgotten about the transaction, or just don't like the goods that they have. We witnessed everything. When you receive a bill, you usually only have a few days to respond, so you must move quickly! To get your money refunded, you must submit original order documentation, tracking information, and maybe a wholesale packaging slip indicating the items you bought and delivered. If the challenged payment is a legitimate purchase, you have a good chance of recovering the cash as long as no misleading claims or commitments are made during the transaction.

Regrettably, you won't be able to tell if the chargeback is related to purchase with precise billing and delivery addresses. Most processors will only compensate you for fraudulent orders made to the on-card payment address. In our company, we don't even bother answering these charges since we know it's a waste of time. Before developing your return policy, be sure you understand and respect how all vendors handle returns. If you have a flexible return time of 45 days, you may afford to be liberal in terms of. Only one manufacturer's strict return policy will force you to reconsider the terms you can afford. When a client has to return an item, the process will be as follows: the customer contacts you to request the return. You request an RMA (Return Merchandise Authorization) number from your provider. The customer returns your merchandise to the supplier and specifies the RMA at the supplier's address.

Returns are complicated by the following factors.

Fees for restocking

The majority of vendors may levy a restocking fee, which is a price for returning an item. We highly suggest the provider not be a part of your return policy, even if these costs are charged. They appear to be out of date and friendly to the consumer. Even if you have to pay a charge here and there, you will most likely have more consumers who want to do business with you.

Faulty material

The only thing worse than receiving a damaged item is having to pay more shipping to return it! Many businesses that sell damaged merchandise will not pay for return postage. They did not create the model in their imaginations to shield themselves from liability for flaws. I see it as a retail marketing opportunity. Nonetheless, if you want to develop a trustworthy business, you should ALWAYS reimburse the return delivery expenses for defective items to your clients. Once upon a time, this was a charge you couldn't pass on to anyone, but it's now part of the cost of running a professional shipping firm. Unless you have a UPS or FedEx account, printing prepaid mailing labels for consumers might be difficult, so you may need to pay return postage to reimburse them for out-of-pocket charges. You should reimburse them whatever, but you do. If the faulty item is relatively inexpensive, it frequently makes sense to mail the consumer merely a new product and not ask them to return the old one. When compared to returning an outdated item, it has various advantages, including being more cost-effective, as it makes no sense to spend $10 to return an item that cost the wholesaler just $12. You will receive a net credit of $, but the customer, supplier, and workers will receive no benefit from this issue.

- **Astounded** – How frequently do businesses ship a new product without returning an old one? Never, ever fast! Never easy!
- You'll get a lot of points and maybe a long-term customer. The consumer will purchase the new product much faster than if the old product had to be returned to the retailer before the new product could be supplied.
- **Your provider may pay for shipment** — while providers do not reimburse shipping on a damaged product, the majority will pay to replace the customer. Most providers will negotiate the provision of a replacement product that you must purchase separately since they will pay for the return shipment. Furthermore, many people can deal with the issue of return delivery.
- If a customer returns a non-default product for a refund, most businesses will ask the buyer to pay for the return freight. This seems like a decent solution. If you're able, you'll surely stand out, and companies like Zappos have made it a part of their unique business strategy

to give free returns on everything. However, it may be costly, and most consumers agree that the shipping expenses of the refund should not be borne solely by the buyer because they purchased a product that they eventually did not want.

Shipping issues

Estimating shipping charges for merchant drop shippers may be a nightmare.

With so many different shipping items from diverse regions, calculating shipping charges for purchases is challenging. There are three types of shipping prices available: real-time pricing– in this case, the shopping cart utilizes the total weight of all purchased products as well as the destination to provide a real-time estimate. This is pretty precise; however, it is tough to compute for many warehouse shipments.

- **Tariffs based on type**– Depending on the type of product you purchase; you can choose flat delivery prices. All tiny widgets are supplied for a flat charge of $5, whilst all big widgets are transported for a flat rate of $10.
- **Flat-rate Shipping**- As the name suggests, you will charge a single flat fee for all shipments, regardless of size or kind. A free delivery may even be offered on all orders. This is the easiest way to implement, although it is less accurate than actual shipping prices.

It is critical to follow the key drop shipping guidelines established at the beginning of this chapter while shipping. We'd want to discover a solution that prioritizes simplicity over excellence, especially since we're just getting started. Most merchants spend days or weeks trying to set up automated transportation procedures for a shop that has yet to be properly sold. Rather, they should concentrate on other issues such as marketing and customer service, and quickly implement a worldwide shipping strategy. As they expand, they will be able to invest in a more precise system. This strategy will frequently increase the calculation of an average delivery cost and turn it into your total flat charge. You're going to lose money on some orders but make it upon others.

Would you want to build a system that shifted additional shipping fees based on the supplier's location if you could? Many customers are subjected to exorbitant shipping costs, especially if they believe their order came from a single location. Instead, try to limit multiple shipments by selecting and utilizing overlapping provider inventory. This is a far more practical and straightforward long-term solution.

International shipping has gotten faster, but domestic shipping is still slow. If you are shipping internationally, you must consider and/or deal with: different weight and length requirements for different countries. Suppliers may charge additional fees for international order processing. Additional fees for the settlement of complicated orders as a result of higher freight costs Excessive shipping costs for large and/or heavy products Is it worth the trouble? This depends on the demand and the profits you gain.

If you sell small items with higher margins, the expanded market can help you deal with the trouble and cost of offering international shipments. The additional benefit is not worth the cost and discomfort for others– especially traders who sell larger or heavier products. Choose a carrier to choose the best carrier because it can save you a lot of money. The biggest decision you have to make between UPS / FedEx and the United States in the United States. Email service. Email service.

- UPS / FedEx-These privately run giants are excellent to ship large, heavy packages domestically. Our prices for large shipments will be considerably lower than those paid by the sups.
- U.S. Postal Service–If you are shipping tiny, lightweight items, you cannot exceed the rates charged by USPS. After drop shipping prices, the lowest UPS delivery price will probably be around $10, while you can also ship products for s$5 or less through the post office. The post office is usually a better option for sending foreign shipments, particularly smaller ones.

When establishing your shipping options ("Within five days" or "Within three days," try categorizing them by shipping time because that allows you stop choose the carrier that is most affordable for each order and delivery time. Take it from us: it's NOT convenient to handle all of your customer emails, requests, and returns in an Excel spreadsheet. As large as Excel is, customer support is not designed to meet these criteria. Likewise, as the company and the team grow, handling aid with a single e-mail address often breaks down and leads to problems and service gaps.

Implementing a help desk is one of the best things you can do to ensure quality service for your customers. Help desk software comes in a number soft ways, but they all provide a single platform to handle your contacts and customer support issues. Many offices encourage team members to assign problems and maintain contact history between all related parties.

- **Help Scout**– Help Scout handles each thing like an email and eliminates all the typical ticket information that consumers see with requests for help, which is less cluttered than any other desk. Instead, service tickets function as regular emails to customers, providing a more personalized experience.
- **Zendesk**– Zendesk provides several tools and integrations that are highly customizable, powerful and one of the most popular support centers. It takes some adjustment, but it is very powerful once it is adjusted to your business.

Desk–Backed by the well-known Salesforce, Desk's Virtual Inbox enables you to communicate on multiple platforms with your customers from a seamless platform.

Kayako–Kayako provides an all-in platform that incorporates traditional ticket service with digital live chat, telephone calls, and remote problem management.

It can be a tough decision to decide whether to provide telephone support. It is a great way to provide support in real-time, but it is one of the costliest support methods. When you bootstrap a business from 9 to 5, calls can not to be treated. Nonetheless, if you work in your company full-time–or if you have an employee who can–this could be a viable option. You will always be able to get your telephone number to voicemail and respond to customer calls later if you cannot staff the phone all day long. This solution sis not optimal, but a successful balance can be achieved.

While thinking about how to provide telephone support, consider the type of products that you are going to offer. If you're a diamond shop selling s$1000 to $5000 in jeweler, many customers won't be comfortable placing a big order without talking to a real person. Nevertheless, if you sell products between $25 and $50, most visitors would feel comfortable purchasing without telephone support, if you have created a professional website rich in detail.

You can find creative ways to do this when you plan to provide telephone support. When a big 800 number appears on the top of each list, low-value telephone calls cost more than they are worth helping. Instead, consider adding your number to other strategic points, such as contact us and the pages for the shopping cart, where the visitor is likely to buy. Regardless of the show, you plan to deal with sales queries, you should always be prepared to call customers to address any post-sales problems. There is nothing wrong swath carefully determining the best ways to support people who have bought from you, but you should never refuse to support them on the phone.

The following services help you to build a free telephone number and sales slime:

Grasshopper– Grasshopper provides telephone services for small businesses. A toll-free number, unlimited extensions, call forwarding, and voicemail is available at a reasonable monthly fee (approximately 25). (Approximately 25).

RingCentral– RingCentral is a VoIP of 800 numbers, and we have used it in the past with mixed results. The flexible architecture allows you to create personalized routing rules and extensions. For Mac users, we recommend that you search for another company when buying a VoIP phone, as the OS sX phone software from RingCentral is insecure and unreliable. We have covered a host of material to date from the concepts of drop shipping to the complexities of finding a niche and running the business.

CHAPTER SEVEN

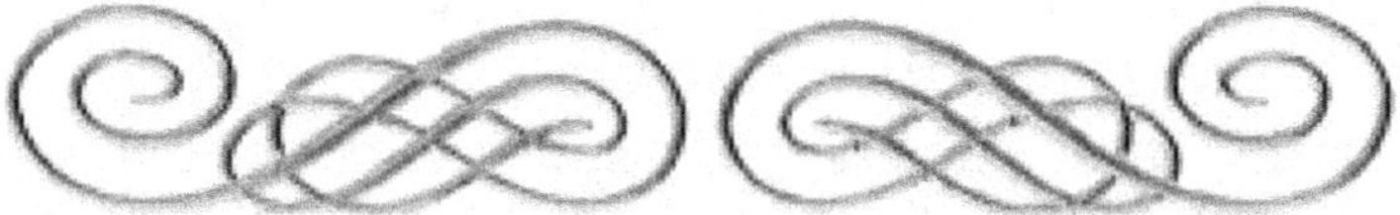

THE ESSENTIAL ELEMENTS OF SUCCESS IN DROPSHIPPING

You should now have the fundamentals in place to confidently begin investigating and launching your own drop shipping business. It's easy to become distracted by learning so much and lose sight of what's truly essential. This is why we compiled a list of the key performance components. These are the primary "must-do" activities that will make or ruin your new company. If you can effectively apply this, you can make a lot more mistakes and still have a good probability of success.

1. Provide added value

A solid plan for adding value to your consumers is the most crucial performance component. This is critical for all businesses but more important in the drop shipping industry, where you will compete with thousands of other "me" shops selling identical things. You would readily believe that drop shipping allows you to sell a product to customers. However, successful small businesses recognize that they are selling more than just experiences, knowledge, and solutions to the services they provide. You believe you're in the e-commerce business, but you're also in the information business.

So, how can you offer value to your clients' lives and address their problems? If you are unsure, go back and study the preceding chapters, which cover the subject in full. If you are unable to answer this question for a certain niche, you may want to consider moving on to another market. If expertise and feedback on quality cannot offer value, the only thing on which you can compete is pricing. Even though this is a successful Walmart approach, it will not help you develop a lucrative shipping company with a decline.

2. SEO and marketing concentration

As a critical success aspect, the ability to generate traffic in seconds to offer value is essential.
The number one issue and aggravation for modern e-commerce companies is a lack of traffic to their website. Too many merchants have worked for months building the ideal platform just to send it into a world where there is no concept. Marketing and marketing are critical for your business's success, but they are difficult to outsource, especially if you have a tiny budget and are bootstrapping your firm. You must take the initiative to improve your SEO, advertising, marketing, and guest blogging abilities.
This is especially vital during the first six to twelve months when no one knows who you are. For at least 4 to 6 months following your debut, you must devote at least 75% of your time to advertisements, SEO, and traffic generation–yes, 4 to 6 months! Once you've established a solid marketing foundation, you may take a step back and evaluate your efforts. Nonetheless, advertisements cannot be overstated at this stage.

If you are not yet an expert in marketing or SEO, you may start with the following resources and blogs: SEO moz is one of the most well-known online SEO forums. Your SEO guide is an excellent resource for newcomers.
Search Engine Land— the SEO blog is incredibly popular, and there are hundreds of fresh postings every day.

SEO Book– This is a prominent SEO blog for SEO specialists, as well as the location of a private paying group.

Distilled–This marketing and SEO company includes an excellent blog as well as several high-quality pieces of training and manuals, many of which are available for free.

Hub spot Blog Marketing Resources Tips on anything from increasing e-mail traffic to using social networking. Tip for high-level marketing and community development Strong is Seth Godin's blog. Burst Free Brand Pictures-Extremely high-quality product images for well-known hijackers.

Neil Patel's Quick Sprout–A blog mostly focused on marketing, SEO, and traffic development.

KissMetrics.com -

Extensive marketing postings focusing on research, usability, and conversion.

Sparring Mind-How utilizes behavioral psychology to assist customers to manage and sell their businesses.

Copy Blogger–tips on marketing materials with an emphasis on strong copywriting. Online field interviews with active businesses and mixology applications not simply advertisements, but also a variety of valuable tools for young entrepreneurs, such as advertising and early-stage counselling.

Ecommerce Fuel–Tips on how to find, expand, and exchange online stores for a successful e-commerce entrepreneur.

Written specifically for each store owner and tiny shop.

3. **Concentrate**! Concentrate! Concentrate! Concentrate! Concentrate! Concentrate! Concentrate! Concentrate! Concentrate! Concentrate! Concentrate

Almost every notable store we come across has one thing in common: it specializes in a certain product or niche. The more specialized a store is, the more popular it is. You just do not wish to sell the bags. You intend to offer backpacks to people all around the world who are interested in lightweight gear. You don't want to sell security cameras solely to make money. I'd want to focus on gas station security systems. Many people assume that narrowing their emphasis will decrease their possible consumer base and lose revenue. The exact opposite is true!

Specializing allows you to interact with your clients more effectively, stand out from the competitors, and compete in a narrower field. Specializing in a drop shipping service is rarely a poor idea. When you launch a business in a new niche, you probably don't know which customer segment to target - and that's fine. However, when you interact with your consumers, you will be able to identify the most profitable area that allows you to provide the most value. Attempt to focus the business solely on the demands and problems of the clients. Even if you charge a premium, you will be astonished by the high conversion rates.

Remember, if everyone is your client, nobody is. Specialization makes it simpler to differentiate, command higher pricing, and better focus marketing efforts.

4. Beginning a drop shipping business is similar to beginning another value-added service.

It necessitates a significant level of commitment and effort over time. Nonetheless, some people believe that they may generate a six-figure passive income with a drop-out after a few months of part-time work. That's just not how it works. It's also crucial to remember that the first few months are the most challenging. You will have to deal with complaints, problems with your website, and maybe a website launch that will result in no sales. Recognize that it is normal! No effective drop shipping firms were founded in a single day, just as Rome was not constructed in a single day. When you mentally prepare for a difficult start and don't expect to become wealthy quickly, the firm will be far more likely to persevere until it is profitable.

5. The Internet has always been a reasonably transparent environment, but with the recent advent of social services, this is no longer the case.

GET YOUR OWN DROPSHIPPING BUSINESS UP AND RUNNING.

It's easier than you think to start your own drop shipping business, and it has some excellent advantages–you don't have to solve problems for anybody except yourself, and it's rewarding for the effort you put in. Unfortunately, when it comes to launching their own online business, most people think of one or more of these three things.

- I don't have time to manage a business, and I don't have the funds to do so. You don't take much time; most of your time is spent putting up your web business. You can set up a completely functional e-commerce business in less than a day if you were the know-how. You don't require a lot of money because you don't have any stock to buy or large overheads to pay. You just need money to create a website, manage domain names, and so on, and you can get fantastic bargains on them if you go shopping. Okay, a little talent is required, but it's not tough to go through.

- Hosting firms provide packages that include a domain name and a website developer with detailed instructions. You no longer need to be a computer programmer or coder, and you can even acquire the website for free by utilizing WordPress if you choose topics for your blog. You'll need an online store to get started with your new venture. You can't sell your products online unless you have an internet store. Customers see where their things are purchased through the internet shop; they don't see what happens behind the scenes, and they don't know much about it either. Your online store should be easy to use for your clients, as well as visually appealing and welcoming. Previously, coding was the only method to create a website. While you may still utilize code to create a website and make it fully your own, there are alternative ways. The procedure is now almost entirely automated, and these are the steps you'll follow to set up a WordPress website (WordPress is one of the easiest to get started with).

⬚ Purchase a domain name and set up your hosting package. A domain name is how potential users will find you and the website on which you have worked so hard. Because the Internet is based on IP addresses rather than domain names, each web server must use a domain name application to translate the domain name into an IP address. A good domain name makes your website far more accessible to your clients. The domain name in the www URL, for example, is "WordPress.com."

The dominating domain name is "WordPress," with the suffix ".com."

Numerous extensions are available, including.com for enterprises,.org for organizations, Mobi for mobile websites, .net for businesses and organizations alike, and. me for personal initiatives. If you want a domain that is only related to the United States, Us is available, and.ca is available to Canadians. You can acquire free hosting and a low-level domain name, but you won't be able to solve the difficulties. Choosing the correct domain name and hosting bundle is the greatest approach to having your website displayed on search engines. When it comes to domain names, bear in mind that the name must be essential to your organization.

⬚ The name must be basic and brief.

⬚ The name must be one that you are familiar with.

⬚ The name should be professional—most hosting companies will verify domain name availability for you. The ideal extension for a company is.com.

This is one of the most popular extensions, but it is also the most expensive to register. Nonetheless, if your firm is promoted by word of mouth, most individuals would type in if they just knew your organization's name. Another option is to choose a less expensive variant, such as as.net, and have your domain name flow so that it forms part of your name, such as shopforyourpet.net. As customers share their purchases with others, rhyme and flow make the extension part of the moniker. It is often a good idea to report on more than one extension of your organization. For example, if your website is awesomeshirts.com, you should also consider registering www.awesomeshirts.net and www.awesomeshirts.info so that the contest does not fight on coattails with the same domain name and extension.

Because a domain name is not expensive, it never hurts to be careful, especially as your business expands. If you do, you will be able to purchase and park your property.

This refers to your property, but it contains no content to protect it against unauthorized use. This is also a good idea if the domain you pick contains an often-misinterpreted word. When you've decided on a domain name, you'll need to select a Webhost. The domain name is merely a marker that directs people to the server where the website is hosted. This server must be able to run the website's requirements. This is the most expensive option to start your own drop shipping business, but you won't have to waste your money hunting around, and you'll discover some amazing offers if you follow these guidelines.

- Examine user reviews and review sites that are not affiliated with the host you are considering. Check out their customer service feedback to get everything you need to know. Ascertain that they have fast servers in the country or countries where your website is aimed. You may now go to the following step by acquiring a domain name and a suitable hosting package: installing WordPress

- WordPress is by far the easiest platform for developing your website, eliminating any coding and allowing you to focus on the content of your website. WordPress is a popular website for a diverse group of people, including authors, news outlets, Fortune 500 organizations, and even celebrities. WordPress is free and can be used to create nearly any form of the site, including a forum, a directory, a voucher site, a job page, a booking system, a support desk, classified ads, and, of course, an online store. If you choose WordPress as a platform, you may design your framework and incorporate user management and security features by extending its current APIs. This will allow you to create a unique site for your consumers that is simple to set up and use.

- As previously said, your host will employ Panel or Direct Admin– c Panel is the most popular and user-friendly. One of the reasons cPanel is more popular is that it organizes features into categories, making it easier to identify particular features. Many more tools and plugins than Direct Admin are available in Panel, giving you a great deal of freedom in how you set up your website.

- When you sign up for an account, you will receive an email with detailed instructions on how to install WordPress–with Direct Admin, you must click on the "Upgrade software installer" button, but in cPanel, the link will state "Install WordPress with a click." One of the finest features of WordPress is the ability to tweak the core foundation to meet your requirements. You will select and install a theme to improve the appearance of your website and attract new customers. On WordPress, a theme is nothing more than a template, and there are many different ones to choose from–some premium, some commercial.

- Although there are hundreds of theme options, you don't want to pick the first one you see and think it'll work for your company. Before reaching a final judgement on the subject, you will evaluate a few factors.
- Simplicity–You don't want to make a theme with a lot of colors, complicated designs, and dazzling animations. While they may be successful for certain websites, a website that tries to sell should keep things simple and clear so that the items are the focus rather than the backdrop of the page.
- Responsibility–A flexible theme adapts its design to different frame sizes and devices. Because a large portion of online traffic is generated by smartphones and other portable devices, a topic that addresses a significant benefit and makes it simpler for your consumers to browse. Customers may lose sensitivity to other online stores if your topic does not answer. The topic you choose should also be relevant to, if not directly related to, the product you are selling. When selling snowshoes, for example, you don't use a beach theme, although a blue or green theme might be excellent for selling things. Choose a theme and modify it to meet your specific requirements. These are the primary changes you want to make to make the issue truly personal.
- Change the logo to your original logo–this is where the tracking code will be inserted if you wish to use Google Analytics–side panels and sliders–you'll want to alter the theme for content in Google Analytics.

The installation of an e-commerce plugin for WordPress does not include a website but does allow for plug-ins. Select an excellent e-commerce app. Woo Commerce is one of the finest and easiest to use, however you must first install and activate a compatible theme. You will personalize your plugin with data like currencies, delivery fees, and so forth. Configure whatever has to be changed, but pay special attention to the following.

Pages

It is critical to direct your consumers to the information they want. There are eight sites to check to verify that your web store allows for excellent client navigation. Welcome: The welcome page is intended to greet consumers as they enter your shop and to give relevant or valuable information that the client believes you will supply for them. About the Authors: The about us page is meant to provide potential consumers with the information they want and urge them to purchase with you rather than someone else. This page should be both personal and educational. It is not enough to declare that you are the greatest at what you do; you must demonstrate it.

Please contact us at: Customers can contact you via the Contact Us page if they have any suggestions or questions. If you prefer to email from your e-mail account instead of filling out the form, the page may offer a contact form and an e-mail address. It's also good if you have a phone number to add to this list, as well as the hours you're available to work. New Product: A new product page helps your clients to access your new items while also inspiring companies to repeat. Customers may visit your website to check what new things you have for sale.

Top Items: Customers frequently purchase top products. You want to include things on this page that attract new consumers and have high reviews, encouraging customers to return and buy more.

Promotions: These are used to notify clients about all of the bargains you provide.
Privacy Policy: This is a legal document that educates your consumers about how your company uses personal information.
Conditions of Use: This is a legal agreement that governs your connection with your consumers. Payment terms, delivery restrictions, and any other pertinent information are included.

You may also add additional custom pages that you believe are appropriate for your website and will increase customer usability, such as pages with information or news about your organization. Check that all pages are properly configured–if any are missing or aren't working properly.

O Taxes This may vary depending on your nation of origin, but most will specify which tax, if any, will be charged. Check that the plug-in to display taxes at check-out is turned on.

O Payment Settings Getting clients is great, but it won't work if you don't provide them with a means to pay, other than when you pay for your items. If the manufacturer accepts payment, this is not required.

O Transport

You must inform your consumers of the amount they may anticipate getting.

Even if these costs are not passed on to customers, you must configure the settings correctly to ensure that the organization does not pay more or less than it should. This also informs customers about the charges they might expect when their order is completed. You should now have a domain name, a hosting package, and a working WordPress website. It's now time to list some stuff for sale.

The next obvious step is to select your providers, which I will do later. All you have to do now is figure out how to apply this to your specific goals. Make sure the title is concise, not too lengthy, and simple to grasp. It must provide specific information about your product. You must next ensure that your product explanation is concise, comprehensive, and simple to grasp. Ensure that your product kinds, such as the form, size of the delivery, price, item code, and any other information visible to the buyer, are correctly labelled.

Product categorization is an excellent approach to avoid irritating customers. You want to make sure that all of your category pages are clear, well-structured, and do not confuse your customers.

If a product appears more than once in the same category, it is easily discovered wherever the consumer searches. It is also critical to add photographs since most customers will not purchase a product unless they can see how it appears. You may utilize the logos of the vendors listed. Don't use too many images since people skim, and if there are too many to see, they won't notice the diversity. Nonetheless, it is critical to offer a comprehensive product description since customers are more likely to recall a product that has been presented orally.

Make sure you inform the buyer how to utilize your items and why he should buy them. You now have a domain name and extension that you have picked and registered to conveniently route your website clients. You've managed to build up your store with a clear and inviting subject, and the pages are created in a method that makes it easy for your clients to get to what you want without being annoyed. That's all you need to have a solid e-commerce shop up and running to sell your fall. In the following chapter, we will look at how to select the best items.

Your biggest challenge will be deciding on the proper niche and the right topics to focus on. The success or failure of the drop shipping firm is critical in making this decision. The most common error is to select a product based on your tastes or preferences, especially if you want to develop a successful hijacker–what you want, not what other people want. Especially if you are not the sort of person who follows trends or who is often referred to as thinking outside the box. I'm not familiar with the product you're looking to sell, but I can make some ideas for finding the perfect one.

HOW TO SELECT THE BEST PRODUCT

Without a strong product line, your firm will struggle to flourish. It may be tough to determine what literally millions of goods you will sell. The product you select may potentially pose additional issues for you to cope with. Shipping, for example, maybe an issue if you want to sell refrigerators.

Depending on where your clients are located, you may be subject to legal limitations while selling beer. Market research may appear daunting, but it is critical to ensure that the people you contact through your website are interested in your offering. If you already know what you want to sell, you may look at market trends to see how the product is doing right now. Even if you are unsure of what you will sell, market trends might be beneficial. Market trends can show you what things consumers buy or wish to buy. Look for goods that answer the target audience's concerns. If your existing product line is being fed to your market, look for a new and better product to sell. It is also a good idea to select a product that is not easily obtainable locally or a local product that is chased by a region other than where it is already available. Another option is to hunt for a product that meets the needs of your target audience. It might take the form of a new TV program or viral phenomenon.

This is also true for determining a difference in probability. When you acquire a product that many other competitors already sell, you will discover something unique or superior to everyone else. This may be a strengthened product element, a market segment wholly overlooked by your competitors, or even something in your marketing plan. When selling a popular product, make sure to capitalize on this trend as soon as possible. More individuals tend to buy the commodity at the start of a trend. If you get on the bandwagon at the end of the cycle, everyone else has already moved on to the next thing. If you believe you can recapture a fading event, don't wait too long to capitalize on a market trend. When selecting your selections, it is critical to consider product turnover. A product line that changes annually will necessitate significantly more time and effort to guarantee that your product range is up to date and does not contain goods from the previous year that may no longer be accessible.

With a low-sales product, you may invest in a more informational website that will be active for a longer length of time. Don't be scared to investigate smaller product categories and specialized markets. While there are fewer prospective clients, there is also less rivalry, making it easier to reach the top search engines and more advertising-efficient. Your success is dependent on selecting the proper product; thus, take your time and do not rush into the first attractive offering.

To develop a lucrative firm, you must be able to do one of the following: having access to exclusive distribution or pricing will allow you to sell online without having to acquire or produce your items.

These are not easy tasks, and you may discover that you are still expensive since other droppers are always offering the same or similar items at wholesale costs. If you can obtain exclusive distribution, you must find a technique to persuade your clients that the product you sell is of higher quality than the competition, especially if the rival offers a lower-priced knock-off product. This is where your website's "about us" page comes in handy, as it's a great way to share your product's exclusivity. Sell for the cheapest price feasible. If you can sell your items at the lowest possible price, you will be able to steal consumers from a large portion of your niche market! The main issue is that you are condemned to fail since the results cannot be achieved. Low price is not usually the primary motivator behind a customer's purchasing choice. Customers want to spend their money on the commodity with the lowest risk and highest value.

This implies you must persuade them that paying a bit more money on your product is the better option because it is less risky and provides greater value to them. Outside of Price, attach your interest. Consider offering information that compliments the items you've chosen. A true contractor would address issues while also selling things at premium pricing. Make certain that you provide counsel and useful recommendations in your unique field. Your customer service is a highly effective technique to add value to your items that is not reflected in the price. If you can answer all of your clients' questions without phoning them and reply immediately to all e-mails, your web business will stand out from the crowd.

Increasing the Price

This isn't always straightforward, and certain niches may be more successful than others. Look for crucial elements that will make it simple to add value to the material, especially in niches with several components. If a product is made up of multiple separate components, potential customers are more inclined to hunt for information on the internet. It's simple to get a new chair for your office, for example. Unless, on the other hand, you do not want to purchase a whole home monitoring security system, you will want to understand how each component of the system performs and how everything works together.
The larger and more complicated the components, the greater your opportunity to provide value by providing product knowledge and training.

If your firm fits into this category and does not have a product line that changes frequently, you have a fantastic opportunity to create an educational website that explains why your clients should buy from you. It will also help you gain confidence since you will be able to answer all of your product inquiries without having to spend time on the phone or travelling to a store to speak with someone. If a product is flexible or perplexing, you will be able to offer comments and advice on where and how to utilize it, as well as how to adjust it if the option is customizable or complicated. Again, if this product is from a line that does not change frequently, you may simply develop an instructive website. If the customs change often, building an information Centre may be more difficult, but depending on the product, it is not impossible, especially if the basic component of the product remains consistent because the major component information is more significant than the variation.

Installation or setup is required.

This might be one of the simplest goods to select, especially if you're looking for something simple. Go home safely–say, you choose one website with a two-page software installation procedure and another with a thorough tutorial through numerous websites, including difficulties. What would you purchase? The most effective strategy to contact customers is to give the most up-to-date information and guidance. It is quite simple to add value to your product and may be performed in a variety of ways:

⬜ Create comprehensive user guidelines.

⬜ Make a thorough review and product descriptions.

⬜ Make installation guidelines and setup instructions.

⬜ Make detailed videos that demonstrate how a product works.

Create a product quality guide or program… You want to know \what markets your firm is popular and how to cater to the \market you prefer.
You can't put all consumers under the same umbrella–a customer buying a tiny, cheaper item is likely to expect you to come back and get them, whilst a person buying something more costly is likely to ask you nothing else.

CHAPTER EIGHT

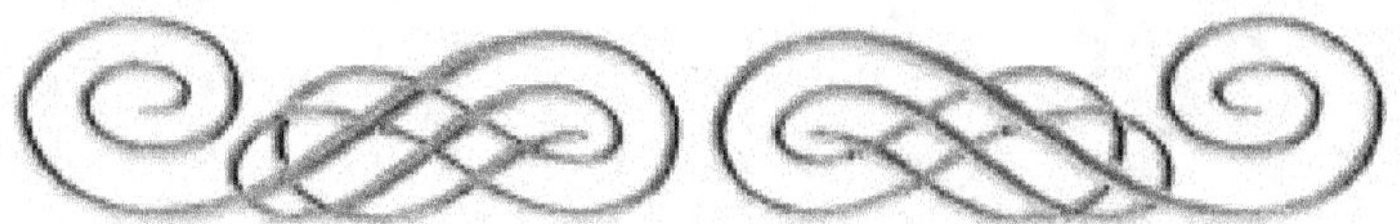

HOW TO IMPROVE VISITATION AND CONVERSION ON YOUR DROPSHIPPING SHOPIFY STORE USING INBOUND MARKETING

- Establishing an internet presence via exceptional content development, optimization, and promotion
- Converting visitors into sales and achieving extraordinary results
- How can inbound marketing help you establish a website and a store?

Inbound Marketing allows you to develop great content to attract prospective visitors to your site and store and convert them into consumers through remarketing and reinvigoration. In this chapter, you will learn about specific inbound marketing tactics that will assist you in increasing your online sales. The chapter delves into the principles of inbound marketing, establishing, transforming, and analyzing traffic and sales.

Increase interactivity and visibility in traffic.

New and returning visitors to your Shopify Business and website will allow you to interact with more people, resulting in more purchases for your store. E-commerce businesses understand this idea and use it daily with a sales-driving visitor acquisition plan. Consider your website and its pages. Is it accessible via product pages? What percentage of your website's material is original? Is this your blog? Do you keep a blog? By incorporating original content production into your marketing plan, you produce strong assets that can be used to attract more consumers at all points of the purchasing process. New, excellent content that is relevant to your items and clients may turn your website into a magnet for visitors looking for, comparing, and purchasing your stuff. The core pillar of inbound marketing is the perception of a website's content as a traffic generator.

Increase your revenue by collecting more e-mail addresses.

Inbound marketing tactics provide ways for generating value for site users earlier in the purchase process. As the procurement process moves from study to purchase, you want your business to be in front of clients as much as possible. If you can collect client e-mail addresses early in the purchasing process through good commenting techniques, the business will be cutting-edge when the customers are ready to buy.

An essential tenet of inbound marketing is to provide visitors who are not yet ready to buy with compelling information and offers that will influence their future purchasing decisions. Visitors will offer their names and email addresses for deals that will provide marketable advice for your business and provide them with facts from your store to make a purchase choice with this framework in place. How do you market to non-clients today? What equipment do you have to utilize in the future if someone visits your business but does not buy? Inbound e-commerce marketing offers a major strategic edge in terms of travel acquisition and remarketing.

Traffic and productivity should be measured.

When you can meet the proper consumer more frequently, obtain visitor information sooner, and educate visitors accordingly, you can better grasp the long-term value of each visit and the specific visitor. Furthermore, by improving site engagement and remarketing, you can sustain and boost visitors to grow sales over time. Do you track traffic from all sources? Are you tying each channel's sales to specific marketing efforts? You will realize what marketing events contributed to the transaction if you examine the complete sales process. Implementing successful remarketing tactics, balancing investment across several traffic channels, and analyzing the performance of each plan allows for the optimization of every stage of the sales process.

Increasing the size of the sales and marketing funnels

Inbound marketing e-commerce assists businesses in filling the top of their sales and marketing funnels. It also aids in the conversion of more website visitors into leaders, clients, and, eventually, repeat consumers. Inbound marketing takes the current e-commerce transaction funnel and improves transaction efficiency at every level of the sales process.

What is the market leader in e-commerce?

A lead is a vital notion in inbound marketing that many e-commerce businesses are unfamiliar with. A lead is strictly defined as a site visitor who gives your site their name and contact information. The lead is anybody who subscribes to a newsletter, registers on your website, or is on your email list. You may have purchased some leads in the past, but everyone is a possible future customer–new and repeat. The advantage of leads is that they may be sold. Because these consumers have provided their email addresses, you may send them special offers, product alerts, and newsletters.

Leads generated by inbound marketing are unique since they reflect someone who visited your website. These prospects are seeking a compelling incentive to buy in the future, which your remarketing may deliver.

Leads to e-commerce sites may be classified into three types:

Tourists who have landed and purchased a product are considered transact leads. So why are they referred to as a leader if they have already purchased it?

These are (ideally) appreciative customers who can be retained for future business. This community's marketing efforts are focused mostly on education and unique offers that will lead to future sales or recommendations. Based on your prior purchase, you should make educated selections about other goods you might be interested in.

Non-transactional Product Leads — Visitors who choose a product and begin the checkout process. You logged in or entered your email address to create an account in your shop but did not finish the transaction. The group's marketing activities will encourage the completion of the planned transaction in the short term, with a return to more deals in the future. Hub Spot and Shopify collaborated to develop a connection that allows you to track and sell abandoned carts.

Non-transactional, non-product leads — Visitors who have not yet transacted but have subscribed to your email newsletter or provided you with their contact information. Such leads are not currently available for purchase. They have shown interest in your products, brand, and services, however, and provide promising future sales chances.

How to Increase Traffic to Your Website and Shop Extending your reach–the total number of individuals who may view the material and items on your website and shop– is one of the most critical growing inbound marketing methods. Higher road mobility leads to more top-of-funnel sales. Even if you didn't alter anything in the middle of your funnel (product pages, landing pages, and remarketing), you'd still earn more sales by drawing more qualified visitors to and from your site.

Use marketplaces and data sources to your advantage. To sell more stuff, you must make your products more visible to more buyers. Place your items in every market to 1) host them and 2) expand their scope. Although each marketplace has its own set of issues for your organization, overall, more listings usually imply greater visibility, which leads to increased sales.

• Each market needs a unique set of characteristics.

• It takes time to manually upload items to multiple markets.

Schedule automated XML data feeds to be uploaded to marketplaces as needed. • If it is not monetarily or technologically feasible to develop an automatic data feed, design your own and upload it regularly. It saves you time and money while yet providing you with improved product exposure. After making a sale on the market and paying fees to that marketplace for sale, you should focus on converting your consumer to another sale on your website rather than via the marketplace where further costs must be paid.

▢ Include time-sensitive advertising pamphlets with a short link to your unique online landing page or store them in your physical packaging.

▢ Set cheaper pricing on your website and store than those found in marketplaces.

▢ Offer first-time consumers discounts on your website or business.

▢ You may utilize email lead nurturing efforts to promote visits to your site or store to the degree that each market allows.

▢ Offering discounts to select current clients depending on their prior purchase habits.

However, before you spend, carefully assess whether the purchase price is worth the admittance fee. When pricing your items, make sure to account for listing fees, actual shipping costs, product expenses, taxes, and processing fees. Then, following a first purchase from you on the market, employ retargeting strategies to convert these marketplace clients into regular purchasers on your platform or in your shop.

Product pages optimized for search

Product pages should be shown in front of potential purchasers as frequently as feasible. Your product pages may greatly boost current traffic chances if correctly optimized. Create a consistent, clear website structure. A simple, easy-to-read URL structure makes your sites easier to interpret and categories for both search engines and humans. Organize product pages as follows:

http://www.yourstore.com/category/product

Also, make sure your blog is accessible via http:/blog.youourstore.com or http:/www.yourstore.com/blog.
This product structure is understandable to both search engines and humans, and it contains significant yet short URL components for SEO. Hosting your blog on your domain will typically boost your site's search ability.

CHAPTER NINE

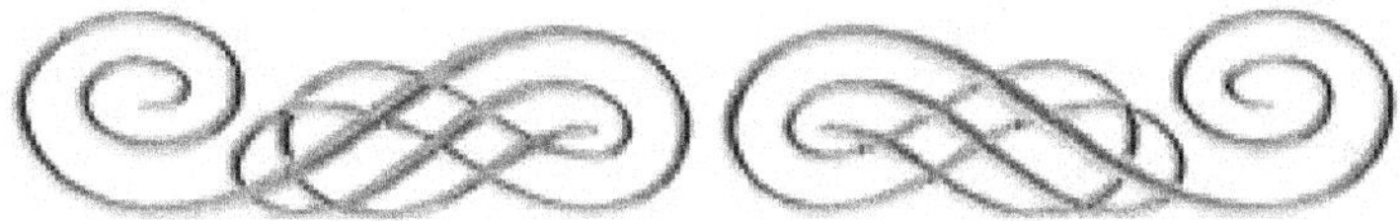

HOW TO ADVERTISE AND MAKE SALES IN YOUR DROPSHIPPING SHOPIFY BUSINESS

Make creative product names.

Search engines diminish the value of duplicate information. Competitors with better rankings utilize the same text on their product pages when you use the same product title like many other retailers that offer similar items online. You might even be fined for using the same copy as numerous other pages. To outperform the competition, you must go beyond the manufacturers or distributor's names and descriptions and build distinctive product pages. Include relevant keywords in the description while avoiding buzzwords typically connected with the name. Include keywords that distinguish the title from those found in qualifying consumer search inquiries. Potential consumers are still seeking product description specifications, so you only need to update yours.

Go beyond the manufacturer's description, as well. Astute inbound marketers do not simply copy and paste the manufacturer's description and frames into their product sites. Take the time to create your titles and imaginative descriptions, as well as to utilize your photographs.

Separate yourself from other stores that sell comparable things if you want to be distinct, exceptional, and important. Such search engines and individuals will recognize your efforts.

Make your personalized graphics.

Product images may be the defining element of an e-commerce store, determining whether or not it sells. Of course, people want to pick something up and touch it before purchasing it. Capture product photographs from various perspectives and let the user zoom in for a deeper look to draw this enthusiasm.

It improves the user experience and generates further interest and confidence in your store, which is critical for this: Add a button to the map. In addition to using several photos, provide an alt image tag for each of your items' images. Images cannot be read by search engines; however, the alt property of an image may be read on a website. People may locate images using image search engines like Google Images thanks to the alt tag. If you utilize product-related alt text, you will locate your items on a different path.

Using header tags

Your title tag (H1 tag beginning with h1 > on a page) should be improved, as should your product name. Because heading tags are vital to search engines, it is important to utilize them on every page, especially product pages, wherever feasible. Using the H1 element to boost the keywords in your website's titles results in an optimized page that can be readily searched for a certain keyword combination.

Use keyword-rich anchor text.

When connecting to pages on your website and shop, use keyword-rich particular anchor text. Use keyword words as internal link anchor text to assist search engines in understanding the content of each connection. By employing good, relevant anchor text, your site's more relevant contents will be revealed and rated higher.

On all internal pages, include supplementary navigation.

Secondary browsing, often known as breadcrumbs, assists prospective buyers in returning to the major product categories and additional areas of interest. They also generate appropriate anchor text for internal links.

How to create an e-commerce Blog

After improving your present content, how can you drive additional visitors away from product and category pages? Many e-commerce businesses are familiar with paid traffic creation methods. By developing original, excellent, and valuable content, you may include sponsored sources or improve current, non-paid traffic sources. A blog is the most efficient approach to generate this sort of information regularly.

What should I write about?

It is a significant decision to write about developing a topic to write about regularly. Create a content plan that incorporates not just your products but also the demands and interests of your industry and customers. Write about how widgets, new widgets, and industry news are used while selling widgets. Don't rely solely on your blog to market your wares. Consider how you might produce newsworthy tales about your gadgets that people will want to share with their friends and coworkers.

Making your content stand out

You will develop outstanding content if you create original, inventive, and valuable information. To that end, don't be hesitant to experiment with video and graphics on your blog using different mediums. If writing text is not your strong suit, consider using video or visuals to write fewer words while still producing widely shared content. Video demonstrations are a wonderful approach to promote items and create high-quality content. In truth, it might just be a shortcut to the material you want to uncover and promote utilizing a different marketing strategy than your competitors. Remarkable content also attracts links to your store from other websites. This generates fresh visitors and boosts your platform's trustworthiness in the eyes of search engines.

Don't overthink things.

Publishing frequent material on your website allows you to drive more visitors to your website and business. It is critical not to overthink or overwrite each blog post to keep postings coming in regularly.

After all, the more visitors you attract to your website, the more sales possibilities you will have, allowing you to become acclimated to creating basic content for yourself. Although the length of each blog post varies, most blog entries should be between 200 and 1000 words. Remember that each blog is designed to drive traffic to your website, build your brand, and be shared online. Although a blog post does not necessarily need to belong, it is typically difficult to write high-quality material in fewer than 200 words, unless a compelling video or graphic component is included. If a customer asks, we say, "What are the top ten most commonly asked questions about your company? Do you have your product(s) available? You now have ten themes for your first ten blog articles!

Users should be interested in your brand and items.

Create your buyer community that is interested in sharing information on your network. Adding a content Centre to your website provides an additional opportunity to market your items and promotions. Using creative content to connect visitors with prospective buyers on a long-term basis.

Taking use of e-commerce for drop shipping Shopify marketing

Using social media for e-commerce chances allows your potential clients to interact on social networking sites regardless of their industry, age, or gender. You should take advantage of social media's rising popularity and join in new conversations to expand your exposure and reach.

Take your cues from your customers.

In social media, your customers are seeking answers, views, and recommendations on what to purchase and who to buy from. The chances of making a mistake in these connected encounters are relatively low. Strategically targeted monitoring of social media conversations is required to successfully engage and lower the signal-to-noise ratio. Once you've learned to listen, it's time to speak out. Your key goals on social media should be to raise brand recognition, measure competitiveness, build connections, and convert social media visitors into leaders and clients on your platform. Begin with the basics — Twitter and Facebook — and then expand your search to include more specialist networks.

Safeguard your social media accounts.

If you don't know where to begin, try Facebook and Twitter. However, for each social media network with which you wish to participate, do the following: • Open an account and optimize your profile • Learn the community's rules, laws, and culture • Navigate the community for brand mentions, competitors, and talks about your goods • Locate tools for using and interacting with a certain social media network; and • Market solely for the market. Businesses marketing in existing communities must recognize that they are no longer on the surface and may need to adhere to community norms seamlessly.

Before being marketed, marketers must first become valued community members and intentionally establish the trust of the community. So, connect first, then encourage.

Pay attention and respond

People prefer to express their difficulties on social media because they receive immediate responses. They employ a variety of venues to collect advice, comments, and recommendations–many of which are tied to specific items. Use this knowledge to develop content that solves these issues and afterwards position your product or customer support team as a suitable solution.

Converting social media traffic into leads

The fact that the majority of your audience is not yet ready to buy is an important issue in social media. Take note that these prospective purchasers are not shopping conversationally, and accept this by providing non-transactional access to your website and store. Then, via email and social media, you can re-engage them as a marketer. Promote social media landing sites that capture e-mail addresses in return for a compelling offer, such as −20 per cent off future members' orders. Only for or − download a Twitter product catalogue. Instead, continue to buy these fresh leads over time so that when they are ready to buy, they will go to your business rather than your competitor.

Keep an eye on your competitors and look for methods to outperform them.

Follow your Twitter competition, your friend's Facebook fan page, become a follower of their company, sign up for their special offers and blogs, and aggressively seek your engagement in and around the blogosphere. The goal is not to imitate your competitors, but to select good techniques and make them your own, as well as to engage in product-related dialogues. Build your commitment and fan following, growing your influence by outperforming your competition.

Capture Visitor Data for Increased Sales Later

Now that we've covered best practices for traffic increase, content production, and product pages, it's time to tackle the middle of the marketing funnel. Your store's major aim should not only be to optimize conversion and checkout procedures, but also to turn no buying site visitors into marketable guidelines. Developing a strategy for non-transactional deals takes time, but it is tremendously lucrative in the long run. The rate of return is twice as high. First, you will convert more website visitors into guides.

Third, just as you would to a new customer, you should point out these guidelines to an established customer. To facilitate your funneling, strategies like calls to action, landing pages, and email marketing may be used. Increase traffic and purchases by including a call-to-action section.

Create action calls that increase traffic and transactions. An action call is a button− literally, an image−that is used to attract attention and direct visitors to a certain website. "Buy now or" add to cart tube "or" Checkout" is a common e-commerce call to action" Please examine the particular purpose of the sites where you have these calls to action: purchase.

What about the remaining 98 per cent of your website visitors who do not purchase after visiting? Take advantage of early-stage buyers' research attitude by positioning buttons that fulfil their research demands. "10 Things You Do Need to Know about Widgets," "Download the Spring Widget Catalog," or "Ultimate Buyer's Widgets Guide" might all be compelling calls to action. This is the type of call to action that attracts and converts the majority of visitors to non-transactional clients.

Landing pages that will undoubtedly convert

When a visitor clicks on a "Call to Action" button, they are directed to a landing page. This page's goal is to entice visitors to fill out a form in return for something they already desired (the guide). Please bear in mind that everyone who views a landing page and clicks on the link is already interested in the site–the form simply needs to close the transaction.

• Provide information to visitors about the value of the proposal. • Do not obscure the visitor with text. • Use bold text to highlight vital information. • Use photographs, videos, or graphics to explain the worth of the offer. Remote the following best practices to increase the rate of conversion on your landing page:

Unless you use value-added marketing offerings like buyer guides, eBooks, and lists on your website, such non-transactional leads indicate crucial visitor information. These sorts of deals also address a huge portion of your site's audience.

Email nurturing strategies that encourage return visitors

You should alert visitors who have indicated an interest in your shop or items but have not yet purchased, much as a former customer might email about specials and new offers. Because each lead has chosen your form and provided you with their information, you have the right to remark on them. A campaign to promote these leads by e-mail will provide the user with a variety of reasons to visit your website. You may stay in touch with visitors and establish your website as a favorite shopping location by referring to current deals and product updates. Email support campaigns should be: To improve the value of a no transactional lead, email support campaigns should be:

1. Provide shoppers with research-based information
2. Push items or free high-value offerings in the middle of your campaign.
3. Distribute coupons or discounts to customers so they may have a plethora of purchase possibilities, therefore it's critical to stay up with your wallets. Use lead diet camps with a strong call to action that leads to your site while also being relevant to your new site conversion.

Your lead nutrition plan will be made up of multiple emails that may last weeks or months rather than days.

Traffic source metering and management

The website and storage traffic should come from several sources so that each visit and transaction can be properly analyzed.

Monitor the return on investment for PPC campaigns, keywords, and lists. Compare organic vs. bought traffic, social media vs. direct, and decide which channel you should spend in regularly. Your effort and money investment in traffic acquisition should be focused on the sources that bring you the most transactions. You'd undoubtedly lose a lot of marketing dollars and efforts if you didn't have start-to-end funnel exposure to autos, abandoned carts, and carts.

Whether you aggregate data from several sources or utilize an integrated platform like Shopify, you must link the data to accomplish more and enhance or eliminate what doesn't work.

Attributing purchases to sources of traffic

The attribution of a single purchase is flawed. Capture early-stage leads, gather information and assign your final purchase based on earlier participation with your site and business. This adds complication to an already cryptic procedure in which transactions are only delegated to the final source of the flow. This can help answer questions like • Are your PPC spending attracting unqualified consumers in large volume terms, or are they drawing early-stage purchasers who return to purchase later?
• Should you invest more in content if a visitor comes from a sponsored search but came from an organic search?
• Does social media traffic finally convert into income?
The long-term worth of each traffic channel can be better recognized if you can record visitor information sooner while effectively nurturing visitors. As a result, you will be able to strengthen your marketing efforts.
However, it is critical to evaluate traffic in conjunction with early indicators of a visitor's buying intents since a hit website is insufficient and a purchase is too late.

Abandoned Carts

E-commerce sites lose a significant number of buyers who are interested in the checkout procedure. Most e-commerce sites lose nearly half of their potential consumers during the transfer of an email address to the final checkout page. When we view cart drops as "leads" rather than "visitors who did not buy," we open up a slew of new possibilities.
• Cart abandoners have demonstrated the highest amount of purchasing intent without actually purchasing • Carts are frequently abandoned for reasons unrelated to a lack of purchasing merchandise
• You've already collected their name and email address, and you may contact them with an irresistible offer. Cart dropouts that contain a small email message such as "you've left in your cart, we'll hold it in 24 hours," which might be useful for visitors who have mistakenly abandoned their cart or simply need a discreet reminder.
Free delivery incentives, a few dollars off, or additional points of loyalty might entice price-conscious customers to purchase. These are only two examples of how visitors who abandon carts might be converted into paying clients. To successfully pick up carts, an analytical system that measures visits, cart abandonments, and customers is required. Each achievement should be examined and replicated.

Whether you utilize email remarketing, update the checkout process, or improve product pages, the changes can always be connected to real sales, and the revenue-based ROI of your modifications can be calculated. The same method applies to high-level traffic origins as well as non-traffic lines. The purpose of upgrading your e-commerce site is to enhance revenue using tried-and-true approaches. The identification of revenue-generating variables and investments in the most successful will boost your bottom line: do more, do less. You can easily minimize client acquisition expenses by reviewing each step of your marketing and sales process regularly.

Begin Your Inbound Marketing Campaign

This book will undoubtedly teach you the finest strategies for inbound marketing for e-commerce. Are you ready to begin? See the checklist below for a reduced version with practical steps:

1. Create eye-catching product pages. The product pages are the most significant aspect of your shop. Make sure they are both one-of-a-kind and spectacular.
2. Increase the store's visibility. Use social media and marketplaces to reach out to more potential buyers.
3. Using Lead Nurturing to lower marketplace fees and purchase costs by sending out timely emails that persuade marketplace shoppers to buy from your business.
4. Create a blog. Create a blog. Remember that your blogging platform is far less important than your content. People like to read information two or three days a week.
5. Make a transaction without using a credit card. This might be a newsletter, a buyer's guide, a checklist, or a cheat sheet. Keep it interesting and encouraging.
6. Place your offer on the landing page. For visitors who are not ready to buy, keep the page form brief and capture visitor information.
7. Provide a link to your destination's landing page. Connect your offer to the call-to-action button. Help prospective buyers who aren't ready to buy locate relevant information, and add non-transacted connections to your email list.
8. Fine-tune the funnel on your feet. Reduce the friction associated with your funnel purchase. Please keep in mind that purchases do not always happen on the initial visit and that non-transactional traffic is utilized.
9. Implement a cart drop-off program me. This campaign targets a high-value traffic segment. They cannot, under any circumstances, decline to provide updates and chances.
10. Keep track of everything and assign customers to the source of their traffic. Actively analyses these data to lower your client acquisition expenses.

Do you want to know how to draw more customers to your store?

Let's be honest with ourselves: numerous vendors struggle with Facebook marketing. Why is this? Because the way they go about it with Facebook advertisements is just WRONG! And it's unfortunate, and I don't want you to end up in this horrible pool.

CHAPTER TEN

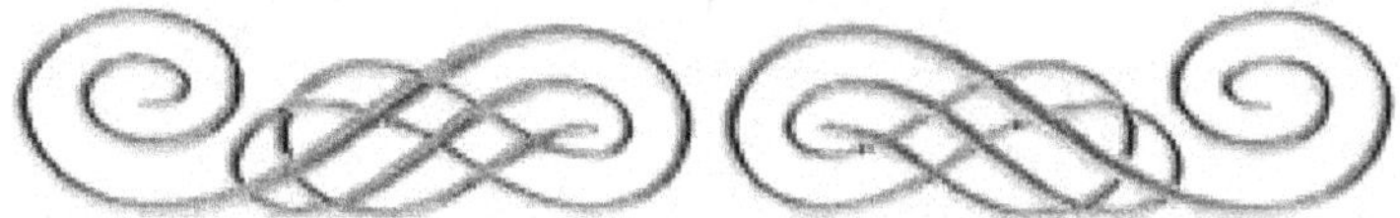

DROPSHIPPING RISKS AND DRAWBACKS

pproximately half of all start-ups fail during the first year of operation, however, it is feasible to avoid being one of those statistics. There is a lot to do to avoid becoming another tried and failed business. If you understand how most businesses fail, you can avoid falling into any of these traps and increase your chances of success. The first step towards avoiding failure is to plan well. You'll be going through some difficult times, and it won't be easy with both current and new enterprises.

No matter how long you work for the firm, you will almost certainly encounter certain issues regularly; the first year is fantastic to practice for the rest of your career. You may undoubtedly discover the appropriate route through the challenges if you have a clear strategy in place and approach from the right direction. If you accomplish this well, your firm will emerge as a formidable front-runner, far beyond your expectations. To create an effective strategy that will keep your company running, you must be aware of the issues that many entrepreneurs' experiences, which end up putting them on a lengthy list of failing businesses.

They must also determine how many other companies will keep them from experiencing the same troubles they have. When you start your drop shipping business, you must be completely aware of the following risks:

Supplier Dependence

You are still reliant on those suppliers, no matter how carefully you follow all of the instructions, standards, and sources from several distinct vendors. We have the stock and can deliver it to your consumers within your deadline. Once your order has been sent on to the manufacturer, you won't be able to control how anything happens. It works most of the time easily, but if something goes wrong, you confront an irate client, a consumer who may harm your credibility. In rare circumstances, your manufacturer encounters difficulty and is unable to reach the standards your consumers want, and it is critical to have a plan in place to deal with irate customers. By having a strategy in place to compensate an unsatisfied customer, you can ensure that you please the client before they can spread any negative evaluations about your organization and instead focus the consumer on the wonderful customer service they give. Don't only point the finger at the service provider.

Many customers will not accept this as an acceptable reason for mistakes. You have faith that your product will be paid for. Blaming the supplier will make you appear untrustworthy and criminal. Excuse yourself for the error and propose a solution. You must establish arrangements with several suppliers to guarantee that you have access to the things you require when you need them. You should not, however, fall into the trap of advertising every item from every supplier on your website. If you do this, you face the possibility of a customer purchasing many goods, each from a separate vendor, making the process cumbersome and costly. One option is to create a separate website for each supply and try to stick to one supplier when you first start - it will cost you, and you want to maintain it until you're established. More than one vendor can be found on one platform, and buyers can order from either. It does, however, require you to be cautious of stock levels. You must manually choose, transmit, and pay additional charges to complete the order.

One safe strategy to avoid this is to limit the additional inventory lists to the core product items that will not cost you anything more. Try to restrict it to items that will let you enough money to cover shipping. If you want more than one supplier right away, you might attempt to choose one that offers the same items as you so that you can use one as a backup if and when required. If the commodity is really popular and frequently out of supply, you may want a backup provider.

You completely rely on your supplier to order, and keeping track of the merchandise while it is being delivered by your supplier will be difficult, if not impossible.

This may generate issues because your company will not appear professional, and your consumer will be unable to trace their order. As a result, customers may now question the entire transaction because order monitoring is now a standard feature of every purchase. Because more products are missing than usual at busy times of the year, such as Christmas, this type of problem will cause much more problems. Several approaches may be used to remedy this issue. One option is to send all shipments to clients on your behalf.

This implies that the manufacturer is responsible for the product's packing as well as contacting the shipping company with whom you have agreed to convey the product to your client. This allows you to track your order and dispatch it anytime you place one. While this has advantages, it is a time-consuming technique that may appear to contradict the purpose of running the business through drop shipping. Things have moved forward a little in recent years, and now computerized software programmers may be utilized to transfer supply data between couriers and suppliers. When you visit a store before filing, inquire about their order tracking system. The delivery procedure would be a lot smoother for your consumers if there is a way for tracking purchases. If the order monitoring system is not operational, inquire whether the manufacturer plans to implement it shortly.

Product Distinctions

When you first start a new firm, you are more likely to focus on introducing new items, building partnerships, and using social media. The things you use on your website may not have been altered or even withdrawn by the maker. While it is critical to focus on expanding your connections, it is equally critical to ensure that your product line is up to date and accessible to your clients. If you sell a product that you are unable to provide to your customer, you must return it to your client and explain why the product they believed was unavailable was not available.

This may make you appear stupid and ashamed, and it can do significant damage to your image if clients receive different things or do not receive their purchases. The new product version may be superior, but it may also be more expensive, and a lack of attention means you, not the consumer, must pay the extra cost. It may also fail to perform an action requested by the user. Spending a little time verifying your offer is current is worth sparing you an angry customer, not to mention the money you can lose as a result of the error.

This type of information is simple to overlook and can have major consequences for your organization. If you pick a provider, be sure that they update your items frequently, especially if they are updated or withdrawn. If you are aware, your website will most likely take action. As a result, being notified of product modifications will save you the time that each product has to be checked regularly. If you can't locate a manufacturer that will update their product, try keeping your variety limited so you can check items regularly, or choose another product line to offer. Failure to prepare adequately, or failure to plan at all it is true that thorough preparation is the greatest method to develop a profitable business.

The more precise and thoughtful the strategy, the more easily it can be used when dealing with fresh circumstances and difficulties. Nonetheless, two major planning concerns will put the company in danger. When you fail to plan, you have no idea what hurdles you will encounter, what impediments the path may provide, or even how to get started.

This does not imply instant failure; rather, it signifies that success will be considerably more difficult to attain. Over-preparation is just as harmful as under-preparation. One side of the coin suggests that you will spend so much time planning that you will not be able to deal. You will be so preoccupied with planning for every contingency that the real business will never take place.

You can't do it, and the business will collapse since it hasn't even begun. The flip side of the coin recommends that you should prepare to start the business, but you stick to the plan so carefully that you don't have to cope with anything that doesn't go as planned. It guarantees that flexibility is lost and sales are reduced. In addition to the hazards of drop shipping, certain severe mistakes can entirely derail your business even if everything appears to be going smoothly. Most, if not all, maybe prevented if you plan ahead of time and are prepared.

Pricing

The minimal cost of starting a drop shipping business makes it simple to select. Nonetheless, this is why many individuals are attempting to start their drop ship businesses, and the industry is competitive. In certain niches, the market is so saturated that you won't be able to profit from it. While it is critical to maintain costs low to attract clients, you do not have to acquire the absolute lowest market pricing. The easiest way to do this is to establish your credibility and be renowned for providing more than simply a product. We want customers to know that we give high-quality customer service, aftercare sales, and product knowledge. You may also recommend offering a nice delivery bundle to assist your consumers to have their items delivered faster or receive a free present that entices them to return to you. A solid return policy is a wonderful approach to acquiring an advantage over a competitor.

Price is not the primary motivator for a buyer to purchase a product.

Customers want a company they can rely on to give the finest service possible. Customers want to know that they will be protected if they receive a subpar product or one that is not what they expected. Even if the client believes that his firm is ethically superior to his competitors, he will pay somewhat more. Logistics To live well and manage a profitable drop shipping business, it is necessary to run a lot of websites, several suppliers, and a variety of items.

Nonetheless, you will want adequate logistical help to do all of this. You must guarantee that your system fulfils all of your orders on time and that your merchants can finish their tasks on time. The most effective method to accomplish this is to automate all of your procedures.

A good system ensures that your clients' orders are sent to the appropriate provider. With the advancement of technology, good software can track your merchandise and notify you if anything goes wrong with an order. Knowing that your customer has a problem before they do allow you to approach them with a solution rather than having them come to you with a problem you did not expect. Orders are missed if this is not done, or erroneous information is sent to the manufacturer, resulting in the consumer receiving the wrong goods. The processes involved in monitoring and processing orders may quickly become difficult, and sorting out orders from several locations and sources can take a long time. This inhibits you from propelling the company ahead and expanding your reputation and earnings.

You can't run several web stores without some sort of automated method. All you can do if you try to operate many locations manually is stress yourself out and possibly lose business due to mix-ups and misunderstandings. Similarly, you might spend too much time on the operational side of your business and not enough time on your social media sites. This may be simple if you chat with people a lot. It's fantastic to be ready to answer social media queries for your consumers and inspire more people to buy from you.

This, on the other hand, might quickly escalate past the point where it stops and starts to impair your business. It may appear strange that taking too long to reach your clients could cause problems for your business, but it is true.

Because if you spend all of your time on social media, you won't have time to focus on the rest of your business. Some of the business factors that require your attention include keeping client orders up to date with the manufacturer as well as all of the things on your website.

If this is a worry for you, you should limit the amount of time you need to spend in your company's critical areas to focus on other vital matters. Make a strategy and adhere to it as strictly as possible. Many individuals start a drop shipping business because they believe it is the only thing they can accomplish; they do not want to transition from their original business to their goals.

Drop shipping is a wonderful method to start a low-cost, low-risk business, but as it grows, it should only be part of a long-term strategy that incorporates both drop shipping and keeping your stock. If you adhere to the long term, you are completely dependent on your suppliers and the market, and you don't have much leeway to react if something changes. What if your provider quits? To maintain a decent level of control over your company and reduce the chance of losing it all at once, prepare your hijacker solely to be a part of a larger company.

Many drinkers overlook two things: the first is to copy a product description straight from the supplier or manufacturer, and the second is to adhere to brief descriptions to have more goods displayed on the Website. For starters, extensive, duplicated descriptions of the provider or manufacturer will not get you anywhere fast because your search engines will considerably drop your ratings. To improve your search engine rating, make sure that everything you submit on your website is original and unique to your site. If you are not a good writer, you may ask or hire someone else to do it for you. You could even notice that your customer goes directly to your manufacturer, leaving you out of the loop. Furthermore, concise explanations will not give consumers sufficient information to assist them in making purchase selections. Otherwise, reword the term using the manufacturer's description as a reference. Make sure it's as accurate as possible. If feasible, obtain a sample or purchase one for yourself so that you can confirm that everything in the description is correct and that the customer has no doubts.

When writing reviews, one thing to keep in mind is to make the items readable. Because bullets and line lengths are your strong points, clients will struggle to grasp if the entire content is compressed into one piece.

Put yourself in your consumers' position and think about what you would like to see if one of your items was purchased. Include information in your descriptions, utilize your language, and improve the effectiveness of your descriptions. Check out a Drop shipper before signing on the signed line with a provider to manage your orders and deliver your supplies. Confirm the length of time that independent user reviews have been shared and read, as well as whether or not they are true.

Make certain that the provider you are utilizing is authorized by the manufacturer to resell the items and that the consumers are not offering a knock-off of the product. Another thing to look for is that they are producers rather than personal shipwrecks.

Logistics would be a huge headache if you route your orders through another drop shipper. Aside from not being able to control the quality of your items, you will also be unable to compete with your clients on pricing. All you want to do is add more prices to the goods, and your clients will most likely avoid your firm entirely because the product is cheaper elsewhere.

Inquire about a physical address or a web address to prevent utilizing another drop shipping service. If it brings you to a store like yours, it's not a dealer. Take your time and place your first order of test products. It demonstrates how well you serve your customers and how effectively you operate. This might be the most important element of the procedure, and you can't rush it. It cannot be overstated how essential the supplier you pick to sell items to your customers is to your business, and you must ensure that you choose someone who will help your business rather than cause more issues for you. Inventory levels and back-order systems must be equipped with a storage system that assures quality and availability, regardless of which firms you choose to deal with. It means your website is always up to date, and your inventory and availability are always correct. That means you won't have to tell your consumers to wait for their item since it's not in stock. At this point, the last thing you want to do is begin placing items on back-order. When it comes to a back-ordered item, you only have two alternatives, and neither is acceptable for you or your client. One option is to keep the customer's money and notify them when the item is back in stock that you have it reserved for them. This is problematic since there are rules that restrict you from keeping the consumer's money for an extended period. If this period coincides with when the goods are on sale, you must refund the cost of the product that the buyer later receives.

Another option is to refund the buyer's money and notify them when the item is back in stock, should they desire to do so. Not only are you confronted with the inability to sell, but the logistics involved are also a nightmare, making the process tough. A consumer may potentially suffer a loss as they wait for an order over which you have no control and may have forgotten. Not doing anything is the best way to tarnish your reputation. As a result, it is critical to maintaining your product listings up to current. Running an online store that leverages drop shipping is not without risks and problems.

Preparing for the complexity of functioning as a middleman between a consumer and a supplier is critical to your success. It is critical to recognize any difficulties that might lead to you losing money and clients to be prepared and eventually shut down your firm. Some of these items are obvious, such as merchandise, knock-offs, and missed shipments. Others are less obvious but vital to your business's success, such as spending too much time on social media and not enough time on product descriptions.

Examine the provider and have open lines of communication open with them, and don't be scared to ask questions. You just want to choose them, and they should be prepared to respond to any requests you may have to persuade you to choose them above any other supplier. Once you've identified all potential downtimes and risks to your business, you can prepare to avoid them before they become a major problem.

CONCLUSION

While drop shipping might provide you with the ideal chance to start a business, especially if you have little in terms of cash and experience, it should not be viewed as a quick way to make money. To succeed, you must handle it like any other business opportunity–with dignity. Yom must have a clear plan in place and must agree on reasonable targets. If you have a single primary goal, it might be beneficial to divide it into several smaller goals that can be fulfilled weekly or monthly. This is critical in determining whether or not the firm will thrive. Instead, if you don't see where you want to stay, you should reconsider your location and all of your choices about your strategy and how the firm is progressing. You can also modify your strategy as needed. Drop shipping is one of the most competitive business models, and without the heavy rivalry of well-established enterprises, it might be tough to choose the proper market and the right items.

If you find yourself in this situation but do not want to move markets or product lines, you must examine the best option. You should provide clients with services that your top rivals cannot. Many things may be learned from your rival by looking at the places where they are active, where they receive the best results, and what marketing methods they utilize. Examine challenging rivals to see what they do correctly and what they do wrong–this will teach you how to do more or something different than what they do, something that offers value to your clients.

If a consumer feels he or she can get better value from you, he or she will buy from you, and you can simply steal customers. Drop shipping is an excellent option to establish a low-cost business, but it has a reduced profit margin. If you want to compete with merely a drop shipping service, you must have a high number of purchasing customers or a diverse product line with each product purchased by consumers. You may utilize social media to build interest in your products and marketing methods.

A drop shipping firm works well with traditional marketing. With this book, I've attempted to provide you with a better grasp of Shopify drop shipping and what it entails. The ultimate secret to success is how you deal with people and how well you provide customer service. That is what distinguishes you from everyone else in your field. It is critical to be wary of phone providers and frauds.

Newcomers to the drop shipping sector might easily become victims of fraudsters and lose money quickly and frequently if they do not conduct adequate research. If a drop shipping supplier requests payment before or every month, avoid them since they are most likely phone and simply interested in your money. There will be multiple fraudsters for every genuine organization, but as you are aware, the actual fees to start your business are little. All you will have to pay for is the cost of setting up and hosting your website. If ordered, not until the entire product has been paid for, which is when the consumer puts an order with you.

Your drop shipping business will thrive if you keep the lines of communication open, stay in contact with consumers, and cultivate positive connections. They may trust you if they wish to return and tell others about you.

Make sure your customer contact asks what you can do for them and what you can offer in terms of value, as this will help you maintain your reputation. You must also keep in communication with your suppliers–if you have a solid connection with them, it will be simpler to deal with any difficulties, such as incomplete or wrong orders. You may also be able to take advantage of special price offers, reasonable discounts, or first call on merchandise if the availability is limited. I'd want to thank you for allowing me to obtain this book. I hope it inspired you to realize that you can start a business with minimal money and become a successful drop shipper.

Despite the fierce competition, you still have viable niches and items that will provide you with a high return. Make certain that your specialization is well understood and that your audience is well established. Although drop shipping does not expose you too many of the risks associated with typical e-commerce businesses, it can still fail and cost you money. With a lot of hard work and expertise, you may develop a great firm and utilize it as a springboard to the future.